WILL JAPAN R

AEI-Hoover
policy studies

The studies in this series are issued jointly
by the American Enterprise Institute
for Public Policy Research and the Hoover
Institution on War, Revolution and Peace.
They are designed to focus on
policy problems of current and future interest,
to set forth the factors underlying
these problems and to evaluate
courses of action available to policymakers.
The views expressed in these studies
are those of the authors and do not necessarily
reflect the views of the staff, officers
or members of the governing boards of
AEI or the Hoover Institution.

WILL JAPAN REARM?

A study in attitudes

John K. Emmerson
Leonard A. Humphreys

American Enterprise Institute for Public Policy Research
Washington, D.C.

Hoover Institution on War, Revolution and Peace
Stanford University, Stanford, California

AEI-Hoover Policy Study 9, December 1973
(Hoover Institution Studies 44)

ISBN 0-8447-3114-5
Library of Congress Catalog Card No. L.C. 73-88036

Printed in United States of America

To the memory of
Colonel William Wise Bailey—
officer, gentleman, and true friend

L.A.H.

Bibliographical Note

Among the Japanese sources cited are the three leading daily newspapers published in Tokyo, *Asahi, Mainichi,* and *Yomiuri,* with a combined circulation of approximately 20 million, including morning and evening editions. These are independent dailies with no political party affiliation; most Japanese newspapers tend to be critical of the government and attitudes vary among the three leading ones. In recent years the *Asahi* has on the whole tended to be more critical than the others, although positions vary among the three and among individual editorial writers.

Other Tokyo daily newspapers quoted are *Tokyo Shimbun,* generally more sympathetic to government policy than are the others, and *Nihon Keizai* and *Sankei,* both with emphasis on economic matters. Two English language newspapers also published in Tokyo and cited within are the *Japan Times* and the *Asahi Evening News*; the latter is not related to the Japanese-language *Asahi* referred to above, though both are published by the same firm. *Kyodo News Service* and the *Jiji Press* are wire services (*Jiji* has had the reputation of leaning to the conservative side). *Yoron Chosa* (Research on Public Opinion) is a monthly magazine published by the Prime Minister's Office of the Japanese government and devoted entirely to opinion polls taken by various organizations and media.

Contents

Introduction

The Japanese leadership has accepted the necessity for self-defense. In the sense that the nation maintains conventionally armed forces for the defense of its national territory, Japan has already "rearmed." But the Self Defense Forces, whose constitutionality is challenged by Japan's principal opposition parties, cannot by the Japanese Constitution engage in offensive warfare, use offensive weapons, or be sent outside the country. For its ultimate defense guarantee, the so-called "nuclear umbrella," Japan relies upon the United States, through their mutual security treaty.

The question for the future is whether Japan will proceed to full rearmament, that is, to *saigumbi* (remilitarization), including the acquisition of nuclear weapons. This decision, should it come, will be based on a judgment of the Japanese leadership that national interest requires Japan to break this last-resort dependence on the United States and, in the literal sense of the word, be possessed of "autonomous defense." If we assume continuation of Japan's present political system, the Japanese government would have to consider many factors to arrive at the consensus required for a basic policy decision. These factors will be discussed in the following pages.

The international environment will probably have the most influence on Japanese calculations of defense policy; crucial to such calculations will be a sober estimate of the threat, present and potential. The state of Japan's relations with the United States and with its near neighbors, China and the Soviet Union, will clearly affect the defense decisions of any Japanese government. However, the Japan of the 1970s is not the Japan of the 1930s. No basic policy decision is made

1

in a vacuum; the state of politics being what it is, no Japanese prime minister can afford to ignore public opinion, especially as it is manifested in the elected parliament and through such power groups as the bureaucracy, business, special interests, and the highly developed mass media.

Japan's decision to recognize China illustrates the nature of the decision-making process. Over a long period, a national consensus supporting improved relations with mainland China has been developing, stimulated by the almost unanimously favorable mass media. Prime Minister Sato had intensely desired to effect a rapprochement with the People's Republic of China but Chou En-lai repeatedly rebuffed him, characterizing the "Sato reactionaries" as one of the four enemies of China and refusing to receive Sato in Peking. Sato's rivals for the succession outdid themselves in proclaiming the necessity to normalize relations with China. Yet the leaders of the ruling Liberal Democratic Party (LDP) knew that while the mood of the country was predominantly pro-Peking, deep sympathy for Taiwan and for Generalissimo Chiang Kai-shek remained. Such opinion was reflected in the factions of the LDP; much time and many meetings were required to bring the pro-Taiwan group into line and to establish a party consensus which would enable the new prime minister, Tanaka Kakuei, to proceed to Peking.

Once the China issue was removed from the political arena by the LDP decision and Tanaka's action in recognizing the People's Republic, the question of the magnitude of Japan's defense became the most burning issue affecting foreign affairs to be debated by the nation's political parties. Prime Minister Tanaka found himelf defending the Fourth Defense Buildup Plan which would require a doubling of defense expenditures—at a time when relations with China had improved, discussions with the Soviet Union on a peace treaty were pending, a rapprochement seemed to be slowly forming between North and South Korea, and peace was being negotiated in Indochina. He had to be ultra-sensitive to the widely accepted opinion, reflected in the national Diet, that threats to Japan had disappeared in the new "peace" which had come to East Asia. The necessity to pay attention to such attitudes was markedly intensified by the spectacular success of the Communist party in the elections of December 1972. The outcome of these elections, while not affecting the stability of the LDP government (the Communists secured 40 out of 491 seats), increased the ability of the opposition parties to obstruct Diet action and complicated the role of the LDP majority.

This study is directed toward the critical debate on defense which has been taking place in Japan over the last three years. In this debate, the attitudes of groups influencing Japanese defense policy, of foreign countries, of the omnipresent mass media, and of the public play important roles in the Japanese political process. In few countries is open discussion so rampant and is the achievement of the widest possible consensus so essential.

The essence of the defense debate is how much, if at all, Japan should expand her military establishment, what to do over the long term with the Japanese-American security relationship, and what role, if any, Japan should undertake with respect to Asian security.

Nationalism in Japan, awakened at the time of the Meiji restoration more than 100 years ago, soon became allied with militarism. The pressures of the Western colonial powers and Japanese victories over China in 1895 and Russia in 1905 stimulated national pride and encouraged the strengthening of militarism which in turn eventually resulted in war with China and with the United States and the Allied powers. Japan's defeat in 1945 led to rejection of the prewar nationalistic mythology, a deep pacifism, and a concentration on the reconstruction and economic development of the country.

The Olympic games of 1964 marked Japan's postwar "coming of age." For the first time since the end of the war, Japan could face the world with pride. The remarkable accomplishments of the Japanese people were on display for all to see. Growing national confidence was spurred by the energies of a healthier youth unscarred by war who, although allured by radical thought, could also find satisfaction in joining the drive for production that was bringing Japan so rapidly to unprecedented heights of economic power.

Pacifism did not disappear but, in the second half of the sixties, security as a national problem began for the first time to be discussed. Scholars, businessmen, and politicians argued over the future role of Japan in Asia and in the world. Nuclear weapons, which in the lingering trauma of Hiroshima and Nagasaki had been unmentionable, now emerged as a subject of open discussion. Few Japanese felt threatened by either the Soviet Union or Communist China; still, only one political party, the Socialist, advocated a position of "unarmed neutrality," which proved to be an unpopular policy.

3

In 1970, as the date approached when the Japanese-American security treaty became subject to notice of termination, the Japanese feared riots, disruptions, and a general strike which would paralyze the nation. Although massive demonstrations did occur throughout the country on 23 June, they were generally peaceful and efficiently contained by well-trained police. Victory for the conservative party at the polls in December 1969 and promise of the return of administrative rights over Okinawa had done much to moderate public attitudes in 1970. Although in 1969 student unrest had closed the leading universities of the country for prolonged periods, in 1970 and 1971 the student movement, frustrated by lack of public support and split into innumerable warring factions more interested in internecine struggle, lost much of its active impact on the political scene.

The political situation remained stable with the Liberal Democratic Party enjoying a comfortable majority in the two houses of the National Diet, but the popular vote for its candidates has fallen below the 50 percent figures in the last three lower house elections (47.6 in 1969, 46.9 in 1972).[1] Even so, the opposition did not threaten the continued dominance of the Liberal Democratic Party, especially as the second competing party, the Socialist, suffered from factionalism and saw its percentages fall from 28 percent of the vote in 1967 to 21 percent in 1969 and 1972.[2] Some observers saw possible future coalitions developing among parties opposing the LDP, but a challenge to LDP dominance seemed still in the future.

The political spectrum included a Japan Communist Party (JCP) which pursued its goals through parliamentary means, eschewed violence, and achieved growing success at the grassroots level by de-emphasizing ideology and championing such popular causes as lower prices, lower taxes, consumers' welfare, the cleanup of cities, and protection of the environment. In addition, the Communists had broken with both the Soviet and Chinese Communist parties and could therefore claim with credibility that they were an independent "Japanese" party. The success of this policy was demonstrated by the surprising JCP capture of forty seats in the 1972 elections.

---

[1] Some candidates elected as Independents later joined the LDP, thus raising the total percentage of its representation.

[2] The Socialists improved their position in the 1972 elections by winning 118 seats as against ninety in 1969; however, their percentage of the popular vote was little changed.

Economic problems between Japan and the United States produced irritations over the years but in 1972 a depressed situation in the United States and an unfavorable balance of trade with Japan which passed $4 billion brought relations close to a crisis. In the decade of the sixties, fears that political controversy would injure the important economic relationship predominated, whereas at the beginning of the seventies a reverse view prevailed. The root causes lay elsewhere, but the textile question in the form of an American request to the Japanese to limit exports of woolen and synthetic textiles became the symbol of the frustrations and the lack of comprehension on both sides of the Pacific. The final resolution of the issue, after nearly two years of feckless bargaining, did not alleviate entirely the mutual irritation caused by the long impasse.

The Nixon "shocks," as they were called in Japan, were the announcements of the President's plan to visit Peking (15 July 1971) and the new economic policy which followed exactly one month later. Particularly in the case of the China visit, the fact that Japan had been neither consulted nor given more than the briefest notice in advance brought strong criticism from Japan's public media. Most Japanese, however, applauded the President's effort to improve relations with the People's Republic of China and grudgingly accepted the necessity to revalue the yen. Time must still pass before the long-term effect of these "shocks" on Japanese-American relations can be accurately assessed. The immediate results were renewed doubts over the reliability of the alliance with the United States and renewed public concern about the defense question.

1
The Background

Japan's Constitution—Article 9

The 1947 Constitution, known commonly and affectionately to the Japanese as the "Peace Constitution," is specific on the subject of armed forces. Article 9 affirms, in part, "The Japanese people forever renounce war as a sovereign right of the nation" and "land, sea, and air forces, as well as other war potential, will never be maintained. The right of belligerency of the state will not be recognized."

When the Constitution was only three years old, Article 9 faced a severe test. With the invasion of South Korea, General Douglas MacArthur, Supreme Commander for the Allied Powers occupying Japan, ordered the Japanese to form a 75,000-man "police reserve force" to replace the departed U.S. forces. The Japanese complied. There were grumblings against *saigumbi* then, but MacArthur, whom rumor credited with writing Article 9, had given the Japanese no choice. Circumstances on the Korean peninsula, too, caused great uneasiness among the defenseless Japanese population, who feared overt revolutionary action from Japanese Communists. In his annual address to the Japanese people on 1 January 1951 the Supreme Commander justified what had been done:

> If . . . international lawlessness continues to threaten the peace and to exercise dominion over the lives of men, it is inherent that this ideal (the renunciation of war) must give way to the overwhelming law of self-preservation and it will become your duty within the principles of the United Nations

in concert with others who cherish freedom to mount force to repel force.[1]

Thus, the dilemma of the ideal of the Peace Constitution and the reality of rearmament was born.

In 1951 Japan faced a new development in the rearmament problem. Along with the United States, Japan wanted to end the occupation, but the Americans demanded a security treaty to accompany the peace that would allow U.S. military power to remain, not only to watch over and defend Japan, but to use in the defense of East Asia against the threat of Communist aggression, the nature of which both the Soviet Union and the People's Republic of China had amply demonstrated in Korea. To regain independence, the Japanese government acquiesced in the American demand. The peace treaty, signed by forty-eight nations in San Francisco in September 1951, recognized Japan's inherent right to self-defense (see Appendix, Document 2). In the security treaty, signed immediately thereafter, the Japanese pledged "that Japan will itself increasingly assume responsibility for its own defense against direct and indirect aggression." The armed force which had come into being with the Korean crisis now became imbedded in the provisions of the San Francisco treaty system—the Constitution notwithstanding. The political opposition to the security treaty was more vocal than it had been at the outbreak of war in 1950. The Japan Socialist party opposed the security treaty as confirming an unconstitutional act and as tying Japan's fate too closely with the United States, whose intentions in Asia were suspect in Socialist eyes. The majority of the party's members also opposed the peace treaty because it was in effect a separate peace signed by neither the Soviet Union nor China.

The government did not squarely face the deepening dilemma until 1955 when a new prime minister, Hatoyama Ichiro, promised constitutional revision to remove all doubt about the legality of Japan's substantial military forces, now known as the Japan Self Defense Forces (SDF). In the upper house elections of 1956, bitterly opposed by the Socialists who would preserve the "Peace Constitution" at all cost and strike down the SDF in favor of unarmed neutrality, Hatoyama failed to win the two-thirds majority of the Diet necessary for constitutional

---

[1] New Year's Day statement by General Douglas MacArthur, Tokyo, 1 January 1951.

amendment. No government since then has approached the voting strength required to amend the Constitution, although committees have been formed to conduct research on its revision. Though asked to participate, the Socialists have never graced such committees with their presence. The dilemma reached the proportions of an impasse in Hatoyama's time. Since then, the government has rationalized the legality of the SDF on the basis of the nation's inherent right of self-defense. The Socialists have at the same time pursued an increasingly unpopular policy of unarmed neutrality.

Acceptance of the SDF has grown over the years. In 1956, about 20 percent of the Japanese—according to polls—preferred "not to have any" Self Defense Forces. By 1971, those favoring disbandment of the SDF numbered 6.5 percent of the respondents.[2]

In order to break the impasse to their advantage, opposition parties have attempted to bring the issue of SDF constitutionality before the Supreme Court. In December 1959, reversing the decision of a lower court, the Supreme Court handed down a decision in the Sunakawa case establishing Japan's inherent sovereign right to self-defense, but refusing to rule on the constitutionality of the SDF. In the Eniwa case the opposition made a second attempt to force a decision, but got no further than the Sapporo District Court which in March 1967 refrained from passing on SDF constitutionality as not pertinent. The opponents of the SDF still seek a court decision on this point, and the foreword of the defense white paper of October 1970 expressed sympathy with popular wishes to clear SDF constitutionality in the Supreme Court. The government has seemed confident that the SDF could pass the court test but meanwhile the LDP proceeds, so far without concrete result, to "study" the problem of constitutional revision, including Article 9.[3]

The Liberal Democratic Party has been in power since its formation in November 1955. Japan's defense policies are its policies. The LDP has always managed a majority in the powerful lower house of the Diet, at times more comfortably than others, and in recent elections it has polled about 47 percent of the popular vote. The remainder of

---

[2] *Sankei Shimbun,* 30 April 1971.
[3] On 7 September 1973, in the Naganuma case, the District Court of Sapporo declared the Self Defense Forces unconstitutional. The Japanese government immediately announced its decision to appeal the case to a higher court.

9

the vote and Diet seats has been shared since 1967 by four opposition parties: the Japan Socialist Party (JSP), the Japan Communist Party, the Clean Government Party (Komeito), and the Democratic Socialist Party (DSP), whose 1973 voting strengths in the Diet are reflected by the order in which they are named above. Each of these parties has its own official view on the Constitution and on defense, but none agrees with the government or with each other. All of these opposition parties uphold and defend Article 9; all would alter drastically the form and strength of the SDF. Only the JSP, however, would abolish defense forces and opt for complete, unarmed neutrality. The JCP opposes the SDF completely as long as Japan remains a "capitalist" state, but should she become "socialist" that party advocates some (unspecified) armed force to protect her from U.S. "imperialist aggression." These parties also oppose the Japan-U.S. security treaty in its present form. The JSP, the JCP, and the Komeito would eliminate it; the DSP would continue it, but without a U.S. presence in Japan (or Okinawa).

In spite of the transparently American origin of the 1947 Constitution, it remains a popular and respected supreme law for Japan. Those who would change it have used as a lever to promote their objectives the argument that it was foisted on the country and tainted with foreign elements unsuitable for Japan, but without apparent result. In general, the Japanese consider the Constitution as the foundation of Japanese democracy and feel that to change the "no-war" clause would endanger democracy itself. Public opinion polls consistently reflect this attitude. In fact, the polls seem to indicate increasing concern for retention of the Constitution as written. For example, in a 1952 *Asahi* poll 31 percent responded favorably to a constitutional revision to legalize rearmament and 32 percent unfavorably. In a 1957 *Asahi* poll on the question of constitutional revision to legalize the SDF, 32 percent said yes, 52 percent said no. In a third *Asahi* poll in June 1970 on the revision of Article 9, 27 percent approved revision for that purpose, 55 percent disapproved. A *Yomiuri* poll a month earlier asked a question on constitutional revision to facilitate greater armament. In this poll only 16 percent responded favorably while 50 percent replied negatively.[4] The ratio of disapproval to approval is apparently running at present between two-to-one and three-

---

[4] *Yomiuri Shimbun,* 31 May 1970.

to-one, depending upon the wording of the question and other variables. It must be kept in mind, however, that none of these polls bears strict comparison to another.[5]

Problems of the Self Defense Forces

The Self Defense Forces work under severe handicaps unmatched in the armed services of most other nations. By constitutional interpretation they are strictly a defensive force which will under no circumstances serve outside Japan. This interpretation raises many problems, some petty, like the objection once voiced to stationing defense attachés in foreign capitals on the ground that they were serving overseas. Other problems of interpretation are of great strategic importance such as the limit this defense stricture imposes on convoy or antisubmarine warfare operations in the waters about Japan. Although Japanese support for the United Nations is strong, it would probably not extend to permitting SDF participation in U.N. peace-keeping organs.

In October 1971 Defense Agency Director-General Nishimura Naomi launched a trial balloon, a "personal" proposal that the Self Defense Forces should in the future look for "humanistic—selfless and not selfish—roles overseas in nonmilitary and noncombat fields." Nishimura explained that the SDF might help out in case of natural disasters, particularly in the "Asian-Pacific region." The reaction to Nishimura's suggestion was immediate and explosive. The opposition parties charged that it was unconstitutional and dangerous, revealing the desire of the Sato government to gain military superiority in Asia. Quickly responding to the outcry, the prime minister declared that Nishimura's suggestion was out of the question and that the SDF should not send troops overseas since such action would be contradictory to the Constitution and to the Self Defense Force law.

Japan's experience with military leadership in the period before and during the Pacific war has focused extraordinary attention on the principle of civilian control. The civilian director-general is a political appointee who serves without cabinet rank in a post that spends more of the annual budget than any cabinet ministry except Education. It

---

[5] Public opinion polls, taken frequently and quoted extensively in Japan, are useful as indicators of trends but are incomplete guides to popular attitudes. The phrasing of the question conditions the response, and vagueness of language sometimes blurs the meaning.

11

is considered a thankless job and few politicians of stature will accept the appointment. As a consequence, top civilian leadership has often, though not always, been poor. The civilian bureaucrats who staff the "inner bureaus" of the Defense Agency rigidly control all aspects of the military establishment. The Joint Staff Council, roughly analogous to the U.S. Joint Chiefs of Staff, and the only uniformed body in the Defense Agency, has no command or operational control over any of the three uniformed services. In the arguments over whether the government is remilitarizing Japan or not, domestic opposition and foreign observers alike generally ignore the fact that maintenance of strict civilian control is at least as much in the interest of the ruling party as it is to anyone else in Japan. This absolute civilian supremacy over the military serves at times to hamper planning, to stifle the initiative of military officers, and to act as a damper to good morale and to well-coordinated military staff work. With no likelihood of change in the system, however, the military men endure it with fairly good grace.

The framers of the Constitution envisioned no armed forces for Japan at all; thus conscription is not mentioned, and no government is likely to find it politically feasible to propose such a system. The SDF, then, is an all-volunteer force which, as a consequence, has suffered chronic shortages of personnel since the beginnings of economic prosperity in the late 1950s. The Ground Self Defense Force (the equivalent of an army) is never able to fill its authorized strength. Infantry units in particular operate with fewer men than the table of organization allows. The Maritime and Air Self Defense Forces fare better, but their choice among candidates for enlistment is restricted. Personnel turnover in the SDF is high. Young men with solid technical training in electronics, automotive repairs, or dozens of other specialties find a ready market for their skills in civilian life, where pay and emoluments are more attractive. Since the SDF is not recognized as a regular military force, there can be no military law. SDF offenders are tried in civilian courts where there is no provision for such purely military crimes as AWOL and desertion. Technically an SDF enlisted man can leave the service by merely quitting his place of duty. Some, though not so many as might be expected, do so. Recruitment, then, is a constant problem for all three services.

The rules controlling the SDF also forbid offensive weapons. Since offense and defense are not necessarily inherent characteristics

12

of weapons or delivery systems, it is sometimes difficult to judge whether a certain weapon is or is not appropriate for SDF use. Heavy bombers, aircraft carriers, and the ICBM, for example, are conceded to be offensive and the SDF does not possess them. The nature of new equipment often causes controversy. The SDF has come under fire in the past for adoption of air-to-air missiles, surface-to-air missiles, guided-missile destroyers, and advanced fighter aircraft. The press and opposition parties criticized plans to procure the F-4 fighter-bomber, the helicopter carrier, new missile ships, and to increase the strategic mobility of airborne forces under the Fourth Defense Buildup Plan. The Japanese public has accepted the SDF, but plans to change, improve, modernize, or enlarge it meet with skepticism, suspicion, opposition, and even hostility. The Defense Agency and the Self Defense Forces must spend much time and energy in trying to build a favorable public image. Public relations was a principal objective of the 1970 defense white paper.

Defense planning represents a unique challenge to both the Defense Agency and the SDF. Planning for the forces is done in a fishbowl. Almost all plans are available for detailed public scrutiny and criticism, both domestic and international. Because a sizeable proportion of the politically active population opposes changes in the SDF, every plan and every budget stimulates public political controversy. Within the government several ministries, Finance and Foreign Affairs in particular, exercise a severely restrictive influence on the less prestigious Defense Agency.

SDF operational planning can become an even more controversial issue. The Japanese reject the concept of designating a hypothetical enemy because such designation and related plans were part of the military matrix of the prewar period. Today they are motivated by a strong desire to live in peace with powerful neighbors who would resent the label of enemies. Naming China or the Soviet Union as an enemy, even though only for SDF planning purposes, could furnish propaganda opportunities to the left; yet without a hypothetical enemy the SDF cannot realistically gauge requirements or coordinate plans for defense. Joint planning, already made difficult should plans identifying a potential enemy become public knowledge, is complicated further by the bureaucratic structure of the Defense Agency and SDF, which lacks clear military command channels. Again, the lack of military law, the laxity of security legislation, and the attitude of the

13

opposition parties toward defense make the leakage of secrets a constant hazard. The security treaty presumes coordination of the SDF and American forces for the defense of Japan, but combined planning has been suspect because of the Socialist and Communist assumption, shared by some elements of the Japanese public, that U.S. Asian policy has been one of imperialist aggression. To the opposition, combined planning between the two military forces enmeshes Japan in U.S. "schemes" and proves Japan's "subservience" to U.S. policy. All aspects of operational planning proceed warily with keenest sensitivity to the bureaucratic, political, and security pitfalls.

Nuclear Weapons for Japan

Since the government interprets the Constitution broadly enough to include weapons for defense, there is no constitutional reason why Japan, within that interpretation, cannot use nuclear weapons to defend herself. While present laws prohibit manufacture of such weapons (the 1955 Atomic Energy Act limits "research, development, and application" of atomic energy to peaceful uses), a political decision to arm with nuclear weapons could be made within the law. As an assurance otherwise to the Japanese people and to the world, Sato enunciated in December 1967 his "three nonnuclear principles" which stand as the government's basic policy on nuclear weapons. The principles provide that the government will neither *manufacture* nor *possess* nor *permit entry* of nuclear weapons into Japan.

The Japanese people have had an understandable aversion to nuclear armaments since August 1945 and the double tragedies of Hiroshima and Nagasaki. After the occupation had ended, they began to manifest their reaction strongly. In August 1954 an American thermonuclear explosion of unprecedented magnitude dusted an innocent Japanese fishing vessel with a heavy dose of radioactive material, apparently outside the huge, designated danger zone. The men on the *Fukuryu Maru* were sick with radiation poisoning when they returned to Japan. One of the crew subsequently died, ostensibly a victim of the "ashes of death." From this incident was born one of the most significant mass movements of postwar Japan. The anti-atomic and hydrogen bomb movement began as a largely spontaneous protest against the dangers of atmospheric nuclear testing, but the Anti-Atomic and Hydrogen Bomb Council (*Gensuikyo*), formed to guide the movement, quickly fell into JCP hands, which turned it into a Communist front. The annual rallies in Tokyo, Hiroshima, and Nagasaki attracted officially sponsored Soviet and Chinese Communist delegations, together with sympathetic foreign visitors, primarily, but not exclusively, from Communist nations. The council's antinuclear protest came to be directed against the United States and the West on the theory that nuclear weapons in Socialist hands were good while those in capitalist hands were bad.

The *Gensuikyo* put its case before millions of Japanese for several years by commemorating each year the agony of Hiroshima and Nagasaki, emphasizing the danger of nuclear arms (in Western hands) and the hazards of nuclear testing. The main thrust of the council's propaganda was directed toward abrogating the Japan-U.S. security treaty by playing upon the dual American menace of nuclear weapons and imperialist aggression which, it claimed, was bound to involve Japan through the security treaty in an American-instigated nuclear war in Asia. The council's leftist leadership used every possible avenue to propagandize Japan and the world on the dangers of American nuclear potential. *Gensuikyo* energetically disseminated to the Japanese public sensational "revelations" of radioactive fish caught in the Pacific, radioactive materials found in rainfall after U.S. nuclear tests, and clandestinely stored nuclear weapons at bases in Japan; at the same time *Gensuikyo* promoted protests over nuclear weapons allegedly kept in Okinawa and on American aircraft, warships, and nuclear-powered submarines entering or visiting Japan. The popular mood was receptive: the independent press as well as leftist partisan journals printed the stories, giving them maximum circulation. *Sohyo*, the JSP-affiliated labor confederation, leftist student and youth groups, women's organizations and Communist-front organizations provided manpower for protest action. The "revisionist" parties in the Diet hammered the government incessantly in long interpellation sessions on defense, the security treaty, and atomic policy, all specifically oriented to the leftist nuclear world view, in an attempt to prove government complicity in, or subservience to, U.S. nuclear policy, or dereliction in the government's duty to preserve Japan from the threat posed by U.S. nuclear weapons and tests. The ruling party, not immune to the prevailing mood, sought to preserve its own image and to defend its pro-American policies. Its leaders attempted to set the record straight by protesting the nuclear tests of all nations and by reporting the amounts of radiation in rainfall on Japan after Soviet (and later, Chinese) atmospheric nuclear explosions. The Diet, with ostentatious cooperation from the LDP in a rare display of nonpartisan unity, passed a resolution in April 1954 calling for the international control of atomic energy. Another unanimous resolution demanding a ban on the testing of atomic and hydrogen bombs followed in February 1956. A year later, March 1957, the House of Councillors (the Diet's upper house) adopted and delivered to the U.N. still another resolution to limit the use of atomic energy to peaceful purposes. Government and Diet action (partisan and nonpartisan) reinforced Japan's emotional concern for preservation from the dangers of a nuclear world.

The experience of Hiroshima and Nagasaki in 1945, played upon by the left in the emotionally charged pacifist atmosphere of postwar Japan, produced the so-called "nuclear allergy." *Gensuikyo* played a central role in mobilizing this "allergy" between 1954 and 1960. After 1960 internal strains between *Gensuikyo's* Communist and Socialist membership gradually increased, and *Gensuikyo* lost its united front character. The organization split formally in 1965 and has had less influence since, although it and many of its former member organizations and allies continue to function within the broad context of the peace movement.

In the *Gensuikyo* years little rational discussion on what to do about nuclear arms took place; the issue was treated as a great crusade. Japan made no contribution to international arms control and disarmament in spite of her vigorous advocacy. The failure of the opposition to stop the passage and ratification of the 1960 revision of the Japan-U.S. security treaty (see Appendix, Document 4), the chagrin of the Socialists at having been displaced by the more efficiently organized Communists as the leaders of the united front against the treaty, echoes of the Sino-Soviet split affecting every leftist movement and Communist front in Japan, and the JCP break with the Communist parties in the Soviet Union and later in China, all contributed to weaken the anti-A and H bomb movement as an effective tool for propaganda, agitation, indoctrination, and action. The Japanese nation had spent itself emotionally. The door now opened to a different, and perhaps more constructive, approach to military nuclear matters.

Ironically, the Chinese Communists, who had worked so diligently to ensure Japan's neutrality and to break the U.S.-Japanese alliance in the *Gensuikyo* years, provided Japan with reason to reexamine her

16

attitudes toward defense and to reopen the nuclear question in a totally unexpected direction. Japan, forewarned of China's first nuclear test, reacted slowly to Chinese entry into the nuclear club, but by the time of the third Chinese test in May 1966 the Japanese were disturbed. Contrition, humility, nostalgia, and sympathy had combined in early postwar Japan to induce among the Japanese people a sympathetic attitude toward their Chinese neighbors. Neither China's domestic policies nor her entry into the Korean War seemed to shake Japan's unreciprocated feelings of friendship. Until this time—regardless of attitudes toward the Chinese government—most Japanese could not conceive of China as a military threat. The matter opened for discussion only with the realization that in a few years the Chinese Communists could destroy Japan without reference to the Chinese people. Invasion had been out of the question; nuclear destruction was not. With the disappearance of world Communist unity, the exhaustion of a unified and effective anti-atomic and hydrogen bomb program in Japan, and the development of a nuclear capability in China, the previous consensus weakened and a new wide-ranging discussion of what Japan should do accompanied the growth of the economic means to do it. For the first time some few politicians and citizens openly advocated nuclear armament for Japan. They remained a small minority, but their views could be heard. At the other end of the spectrum, a much larger and more militant minority clung with undiluted fervor to the old arguments for unarmed neutrality and against a bilateral security arrangement with an "imperialist" power.

With the passage of time, Japan's security has become a less emotional issue. The government has come to think of nuclear arms control as an international diplomatic process involving dialogue among nuclear powers at the bargaining table hammering out solutions to specific questions, not as a bold surge of popular will to enforce the destruction of nuclear weapons by the sheer weight of outraged public opinion. Consideration of the nuclear nonproliferation treaty brought the Japanese government face-to-face with the realities of the uses of nuclear power, the problems of safeguards, and the relevance of international controls.

The following chapters discuss different stages in the evolution of Japan's defense debate, with emphasis on (1) developments in 1970, when the security treaty became subject to notice of termination and the defense white paper was published; (2) developments in 1971

17

when the discussion of national security was sharpened by consideration of the Fourth Defense Buildup Plan and the changing defense relationship with the United States; and (3) developments in 1972 when the Japanese government recognized the People's Republic of China, approved the Fourth Defense Buildup Plan, and held elections for the House of Representatives.

There follows an analysis of the nuclear problem and of Japanese attitudes toward the remilitarization of Japan.

2

Defense Policy: Press and Public Reaction

A Basic Policy for National Defense: 1957

The Japan Self Defense Forces metamorphosed into their present form in 1954 in response to an American offer in 1953 of military assistance under the terms of which the recipients were required by United States law to the military forces, not police (see Appendix, Document 3). These forces had originally been organized in August 1950 as the National Police Reserve, on the order of the Supreme Commander of the Allied Powers who sought to protect Japan from possible indirect aggression when combat elements of the U.S. occupation forces left Japan to stem the invasion of South Korea. In 1952 this small 75,000-man ground force became the National Safety Force as a result of Japan's endeavor partially to fulfill the provision of the San Francisco peace treaty which called upon her to provide increasingly for her own defense. The National Safety Force added a small navy. The present tri-service organization came into being with the Self Defense Forces.

All these changes in Japan's defense took place during the tenure of Prime Minister Yoshida Shigeru, whom the opposition parties of the day roundly criticized for violating the Constitution, for rearming Japan and opening the door to militarism, and for failing to consult the wishes of the people in the development of military forces. Yoshida exasperated his opponents by steadfastly maintaining that the armed forces he had fathered were not "war potential," that Japan had not rearmed, and that none of the steps Japan had taken violated the Constitution. It is hardly surprising that under these controversial circumstances no formal, systematic outline of defense policy was ever

19

drawn up. The fact that Japan had nearly 200,000 men under arms in what amounted to an army, a navy, and an air force, and that there was no agreed government policy for the defense of the nation or for the employment of the forces infuriated Yoshida's opponents and deepened the suspicions of many people toward the intentions of conservative government leaders. Yoshida stepped down in December 1954 under a cloud of public antipathy caused in part by his actions on defense.

Under Prime Minister Kishi Nobusuke the National Defense Council (established by law in 1956) finally announced the government's basic policy for the defense of Japan in May 1957. The policy was more a statement of principles than a guide for action and sought:

(1) To realize world peace by supporting the activities of the United Nations, seeking the harmony and cooperation of all nations;

(2) To stabilize the livelihood of the people, instill patriotism, and establish a firm foundation for insuring the nation's security;

(3) To consolidate defense power gradually and within the limits necessary for defense in consonance with the nation's ability to do so and the circumstances in which the nation finds itself; and

(4) To rely on the Japan-U.S. security treaty as the keystone for dealing with external aggression until the time comes when the United Nations can prevent aggression effectively.

The Situation in 1970 (June 23 to Late October): Comment and Reaction to Defense Issues

The 1957 policy continues to serve as the basis of Japan's national defense to this day, although it came under close scrutiny in 1970 during the tenure of Nakasone Yasuhiro as director-general of the Japan Defense Agency. Nakasone, the leader of a faction in the ruling Liberal Democratic Party, had long been marked as a hawk among Japanese conservative politicians. When Prime Minister Sato Eisaku appointed him director-general in January 1970, the choice was criticized by opposition leaders, journalists, and political commentators because of his previous public advocacy of "autonomous" defense, meaning more reliance on Japanese efforts and less on the U.S. deterrent. However, his appointment acted as a tonic for the Defense Agency, the "hot potato" of Japanese politics, for its directors-general had been, with few exceptions, political nonentities throughout the fifteen years of its existence. While Nakasone held office longer than any of his twenty-four predecessors, his record was a mere eighteen months. The confluence of Nakasone's rather strong personality and relatively outspoken manner with the circumstances of the mid-1970 attention to defense considerations led to an interesting news media dialogue on the subject which ultimately reached, and perhaps influenced, a large segment of the Japanese population not otherwise noted for its interest in or awareness of defense problems.

The occasion for discussion was the change in the status of the Japan-U.S. security treaty in June 1970 marking the expiration of the ten-year fixed term of the treaty and ushering in an indefinite period of "automatic continuation" during which either side could obtain release from its obligation upon one year's notification to the other. With President Nixon's 1969 Guam Doctrine (soon to be called the Nixon Doctrine) as background, the Japanese saw themselves faced with some real, and difficult, choices in matters of defense.

The period of automatic continuation meant in Prime Minister Sato's words "an era of choice" for Japan, but the choice was made poignant by American intentions to withdraw substantial forces from the western Pacific—intentions confirmed by action in Indochina, Korea, and elsewhere. No Japanese ventured to suggest that Japan replace U.S. military power in the western Pacific. Such would be both unconstitutional and politically out of the question. Any attempt on Japan's part to fill that gap would consist solely of diplomatic, political, or economic action. But partial U.S. withdrawal, as many Japanese view the matter, did pose real defense problems including such fundamental matters as basic defense policy; size, equipment, and posture of the Self Defense Forces; defense expenditure in relation to the overall budget; the limits of defense power quantitatively and geographically; the relationship of increasing defense expenditure to such important institutional factors as continued civilian control or the danger of the growth of a military-industrial complex; and to such concrete problems as the defense of Okinawa, the relationship with Taiwan, and perhaps the most disturbing of all because of its implication of direct continental entanglement, the defense of the Republic of Korea.

In his November 1969 joint communiqué with President Nixon, Prime Minister Sato announced his government's intention to continue the security treaty beyond the expiration date of the ten-year fixed term (see Appendix, Document 7). Although opposed in varying degrees by the opposition parties in the Diet, this decision had been long anticipated. The opposition had promised protest demonstrations and disruptions to rival or surpass those of 1960 when, despite massive protests from the left, the treaty passed the Diet. But the new movement failed at least partly because ruinous cleavages had developed among the leftists after the affair of 1960, but also because such sharply critical sentiment could no longer be aroused in opposition to the treaty itself. (In 1960 many Japanese were inclined to believe opposition propaganda to the effect that ratifying the security treaty would lead Japan into war as a pawn of aggressive American policies in East Asia. By 1970 opinion had shifted; with experience had come more confidence in the working of the treaty. The United States had fought its war, but Japan had not been dragged in.)

Both the U.S. decision to yield administrative rights in Okinawa to Japan by 1972 and the enunciation of the Nixon Doctrine contributed to a changed atmosphere by easing a deep-seated source of tension between the two countries and placing the defense of Japan in a more realistic perspective. As director-general, Nakasone formulated an attention-getting program to meet the challenge of Japan's new defense situation. Given nationwide coverage, his plans triggered discussion, questions, and opposition on the defense problem, thus encouraging a dialogue unusual in postwar Japan.

As a result of Nakasone's efforts, in October 1970 the Japan Defense Agency succeeded at long last in issuing a defense white paper—Japan's first—and a day later a draft five-year plan for increasing Japan's defenses. In one of the perennial cabinet reshuffles, Nakasone left office in July 1971. More than a year later the government had not yet acted upon the Defense Agency's Fourth Defense Buildup Plan, nor could it agree upon any modified version of Nakasone's original draft.

Let us now examine the content, direction, and possible effects upon the Japanese public of the dialogue on defense from the beginning of automatic continuation, 23 June 1970, through the discussion of the defense white paper and the draft Fourth Defense Buildup Plan five months later.

The press accepted the onset of the period of automatic continuation with aplomb. The hysteria that accompanied ratification in the spring of 1960 was lacking and the newspapers showed little inclination to condemn continuation of the treaty out of hand. In fact, there was more of a tendency to criticize the doctrinaire negativism of the JSP toward the treaty than its extension into what the media liked to call an "era of qualitative change" in U.S.-Japanese military relations. The *Tokyo Shimbun,* more progovernment than most influential papers but a keen observer of military affairs, pointed out the JSP tendency to compare in absolute and mutually exclusive terms the value of the Constitution and the value of the security treaty. But, as the editors noted, there were many Japanese who had come to feel that the security treaty was a protection for the Constitution. The JSP stand on unarmed neutrality had lost support,[1] and popular feelings had gradually shifted from peace at any price to one of nationalism based on Japan's emergence as an economic great power. As usual, however, the press spiced a blandly sanguine acceptance of the treaty's new era with peppery warnings to the government about the limits on changes in defense posture imposed on Japan by the Constitution, the treaty, and various foreign nations whose uneasy views of Japan could not be dismissed. For example, the concept of "autonomous defense" had to be carefully scrutinized in the context of the situation in the Pacific region.

The new era of qualitative change had scarcely ceased to be news when the press played up the disquieting information that 20,000 U.S. troops might be removed from Korea as part of the American follow-through under the Nixon Doctrine. Moderate coverage in mid-July noted that partial U.S. withdrawal from the Republic of Korea (ROK) would be bound to have repercussions on Japan's security. Conceding that Japan had no legitimate cause to intercede, the press observed that any U.S. withdrawal from the peninsula would be bound to add significance to American bases in Japan and Okinawa, especially if some new emergency were to arise between the two Koreas. Again there was agreement that Japan under no circumstances could move to replace United States military power with its own; in fact, many Japanese believed that Japan-ROK cooperation in an emergency could not extend beyond the kind of logistical support which Japan had provided in 1950. Almost everyone agreed that if the ROK should fall, the security of Japan would be endangered, but no one was prepared to face the dilemma squarely. Later articles drew comfort from the lack of an immediate military threat to Korea, and even suggested the

---

[1] For example, the *Japan Times* (29 December 1969) cited the JSP's position on unarmed neutrality as one of the reasons for the party's losses in the 1969 elections, terming it "too unrealistic."

possibility of peaceful North-South reconciliation. Korea remained of concern to those who thought about Japan's security, but in July 1970 the public was notably apathetic. The Japanese were clearly unwilling to take collective steps with other Asian nations to provide for Asian security. Frequently, discussions of possible U.S. troop withdrawals led to the question of whether these might force a merger of the Japan-U.S. security treaty into a multilateral Pacific area treaty organization (PATO), a "reincarnation" of a past figment of leftist imagination, a Northeast Asia treaty organization (NEATO).

As soon as disturbing thoughts about Korea receded from the headlines, Nakasone's proposals for revision of basic defense policy came before the government and the Liberal Democratic Party for consideration and stimulated renewed interest in the defense question. Essentially what he proposed was to replace Articles 3 and 4 of the 1957 basic *defense* policy with a new five-point basic *security* policy consisting of the following:[2]

(1) Protect the Constitution through autonomous defense of the fatherland.

(2) Integrate defense policy with foreign and domestic policy to form a cohesive whole.

(3) Insure civilian control of the military force.

(4) Adhere to the policy of the three nonnuclear principles that Japan, while admitting the constitutionality of defensive nuclear weapons, will neither possess nor manufacture nor introduce them into the country.

(5) Make up deficiencies in the nation's defenses with the security treaty.

In his presentation to the National Defense Council (NDC) on 24 July, Nakasone argued that the international situation affecting Japan had changed dramatically since 1957. The cold war had given way to U.S.-Soviet coexistence, while the Communist bloc had disintegrated into Sino-Soviet confrontation. Japan no longer depended completely on the United States, China had now become a major power, and Sino-U.S. relations showed signs of delicate change despite the spread of the Indochina War into Cambodia and Laos. Japan's internal situation, too, had improved; popular views of armament and defense had become less emotional and Japan's neighbors now saw

---

[2] *Asahi Shimbun,* 19 and 20 March 1970.

her in a different light. All this called for careful reconsideration and restudy of the basic defense policy. Points one and five of Nakasone's plan were a subtle attempt to relegate the security treaty to a secondary role by creating the illusion that Japan's defense now centered in Japanese hands, while point four, supported by five, made explicit the thesis that Japan would continue to eschew nuclear armament while continuing to rely on the security treaty.[3] Point two became the basis for Nakasone's request that Japan establish a national security council which would include the foreign minister and other ministers concerned with such domestic affairs as impinged on his broad concept of defense.

The content of Nakasone's plan was public knowledge well before the NDC met to consider it; discussion in the news media was lively though not so negative as it might have been just a few years earlier. Most editorials urged caution in changing the basic defense policy while they applauded the inclusion of the three nonnuclear principles as a constructive step. At least two influential (and conservative) newspapers, the *Nihon Keizai Shimbun* and the *Tokyo Shimbun,* rejected the changes without rancor, while the *Mainichi*—at times in the past bitterly antimilitary—agreed to the principle of autonomous defense in that it admitted that every nation must assume primary responsibility for its own safety. Other newspapers, however, were cautious about placing emphasis on autonomous defense and downgrading the position of the security treaty. For example, the *Yomiuri* pointed out that autonomous defense was an illusion because Japan held no nuclear deterrent. It also argued against Nakasone's shift to the primacy of autonomous defense on the grounds that such a shift would have adverse effects on China, Southeast Asian nations, and the United States, and would be self-defeating because of the suspicions it would arouse.

In these arguments there was a peculiarly uncharacteristic recognition on the part of the press of the necessity for collective defense, not going beyond the U.S. and Japan as the collective, and of the value of American friendship and the security treaty. The security treaty performed two functions: it was to defend Japan and to help maintain stability and peace in East Asia. The first function Japan might in time fulfill, but the Constitution forbade any action on the second. In

---

[3] For the discussion of nuclear weapons in the white paper, *The Defense of Japan,* see Appendix, Document 9, p. 134.

this, the United States must continue to play the primary role. This argument clashes with that expressed in 1960, and that of the Socialists and Communists today, that the treaty's obligation to the defense of international peace and security in the Far East would inevitably draw Japan into war in Asia.

Another argument against Nakasone's proposal concerned limitations on conventional defense power. His proposal eliminated point three of the 1957 basic policy which placed somewhat vague temporal, economic, and situational restrictions on growth of the military forces. There had been serious complaints that these restrictions were not sufficiently explicit. Now Nakasone wanted to drop them completely. Was he unlocking the door for unlimited defense expenditures? Could this lead to the formation of a powerful military-industrial complex that would promote aggressive or provocative military behavior by the Japanese through complementary vested interests in the supply and demand for arms? Newspaper editorials agreed that the lack of express limitation on defense growth coupled with Nakasone's autonomous defense program, which relegated the United States to a secondary role, was not only a step backward but a positive danger for the country. Nakasone's proposal to break defense expenditures away from a set percentage of Japan's gross national product (GNP) and to link them completely with social security and educational budgetary appropriations did not, in the eyes of the newspapers, serve to restrict the possibility of unnecessary, and perhaps unwise, defense expenditure.

The news media soon supplemented editorial discussion with considerable reportage on the NDC meeting and the reactions of other government and ruling party leaders to Nakasone's proposal. The longer the plan came under scrutiny, the more outspoken the opposition to it seemed to become. Neither the government nor the LDP reacted with particular favor. Foreign Minister Aichi, for example, objected strongly to downgrading America's role in defense as a positive hindrance to U.S.-Japanese relations and as conducive to further suspicion about the revival of militarism. Later it was disclosed that, in addition to the foreign minister, Nakasone's proposal was opposed by the Liberal Democratic Party's secretary general (Tanaka Kakuei), the chief of the Security Problems Research Council (Akagi Munenori), and the chief of the Foreign Affairs Research Council (Kosaka Zentaro). Generally, the objections echoed the reservations of the press, although certain conservatives also opposed the inclusion of the three nonnuclear principles in any basic security policy on grounds that this might bind the hands of future governments. Some press commentaries in turn found this argument as objectionable as the same reasoning—fallacious in their view—that had kept Japan from ratifying the nuclear non-proliferation treaty. Leaving the door ajar for the reconsideration of nuclear weapons could invite world criticism and make Japan's international position less secure rather than more.[4]

By the end of July it was apparent that Nakasone had lost the battle. On the 27th the government announced that no national security council would be established, but that the Foreign Affairs and Security Problems Research Councils would meet together periodically to allow the Defense Agency director-general, the foreign minister, and the chief cabinet secretary to "unify their views." It now became clear that the security treaty could not be considered a supplement to autonomous defense and that the defense white paper would be rooted in the 1957 defense policy. The Defense Agency began its face-saving work on the white paper in mid-August.

Coincidentally, the annual date for national reflection on the Pacific war fell at this very moment. The anniversary of the end of the war, 15 August, is usually noted in the media with commemorative articles and editorials. As the twenty-fifth anniversary, 1970 had some special, added significance. The prestigious *Asahi* produced a thoughtful article pertinent to the nation's quickening interest in military affairs which reflected on the progress the nation had made since the devastation of the war and noted how things had changed—how pride and confidence had returned. The editors, too, were impressed with the nation's immense vitality, but fretted over Japan's spiritual and social environment. They asked how much progress had really been made. Was it enough to bend all efforts to economic improvement? Japan's economic strength, they warned, had again aroused outside suspicion while within, some young people sought to demolish the present affluent structure. Had quantitative increase actually brought qualitative improvement? They agreed that most Japanese wanted peace, but cautioned that foreign nations did not necessarily see Japan in the

---

[4] "Autonomous defense" and the "Nakasone plan" were widely discussed during June and July. Among pertinent articles were: "Government to Reform National Defense Basic Policy," *Tokyo Shimbun*, 20 June 1970; "Limits to Self-Defense Power and Its Strategy," *Mainichi Shimbun*, 23 June 1970; and "Indispensable Conditions for Autonomous Defense," *Nihon Keizai Shimbun*, 6 July 1970.

same light. It was important, they observed, that no matter how much the Japanese may mentally reject war, foreigners do not believe actual rejection to be the case. Japan lives by a constitutional pledge not to possess military power and to trust in the justice and sincerity of the peace-loving people of the world. Prime Minister Sato had told Canada's Prime Minister Trudeau that Japan would not countenance militarism because the Constitution forbade it. This was fine, but had Japan really lived up to its ideals? The Japanese government had endorsed the entry of U.S. troops into Cambodia, and Sato had made a joint communiqué with Nixon. In addition, Japan's defense industries were clamoring for contracts. The editors saw Japan on the brink of losing its principles. *Asahi* then charged the older generation, the leaders of the nation, with the responsibility of preventing economic development from moving into militarism and nationalism from becoming "extreme"; the journal reminded the Japanese that narrow, big-power nationalism which disregards other nations has no place in the Constitution. The *Asahi* editors sounded clear warning to the Japanese people to avoid the appearance of chauvinism and militarism, and to heed the views of their international neighbors, but they did not call for the abrogation of the security treaty nor for a denial of defense responsibility. This editorial probably came close to the feeling of many intelligent, thoughtful Japanese.

The *Yomiuri* called upon Japan to keep the memory of the war alive until a peaceful image of Japan could be established throughout the world. *Yomiuri* gave credit to the U.S. occupation for exterminating militarism, but pointed out that those postwar reforms had the people's support. Japan's liberation from the yoke of militarism had saved the ruling class itself, paved the way for economic rehabilitation, and rejuvenated industrial management. From 1868 to 1945 Japan was ridden with militarism, but since that time economic goals had dominated the minds of Japanese. Now these goals apparently were achieved, at least tentatively. Under these circumstances, what international role should the nation play? Should Japan adopt the stance of a big military power on the pretext of autonomous defense and accede to the U.S. role in Asia, or should she seek reconciliation with China and an environment of peace? Then, almost as an afterthought, the editors noted that as long as Japan backs the Republic of Korea and the Republic of China, she confronts the Chinese People's Republic, thus increasing tensions, strengthening the tendency to reverse postwar reforms, and negating the expensive lesson of defeat.

Hardly had the annual rededication to constitutional ideals subsided when a tempest of a more down-to-earth nature swept through political circles, capturing and holding the attention of the news media for three stormy days. The occasion was the public revelation of testimony six months earlier by Deputy Undersecretary of State U. Alexis Johnson before the United States Senate Foreign Relations Committee. The Johnson statement of January 1970, as interpreted in the Japanese press on 23 August, left its readers with the erroneous impression that the United States would be able to keep nuclear weapons on Okinawa after reversion and that the United States might delay the reversion if certain conditions were not met. The uproar over this news was considerable. The opposition parties, the JSP in particular, expressed delight at the discomfiture of the government, which had no ready answer to the Johnson statement except to say that Okinawa would revert on schedule and that Japan would uphold the three nonnuclear principles there. The JSP was quick to advance this incident as proof of repeated allegations of a secret deal between the United States and the Japanese government which would reduce the substance of Okinawan reversion to a mere shadow. The press, unwilling to go this far, worried that Okinawa would return to Japan without clear-cut understanding of the terms on each side. The prime minister made a statement on 25 August that the introduction of nuclear weapons into Okinawa would be on the same basis as in the homeland, and the foreign minister's categorical denial of any secret agreements on reversion appeared in the news on the 26th. That same day, when the United States assured Japan that reversion would take place on schedule under the explicit conditions of the agreement, the storm abated as quickly as it had arisen.

The general press reaction to the essentially trivial "Johnson-testimony" incident revealed not only the exploitability of the nuclear issue by the left but the sensitivity of the government to assumed popular anxieties over Okinawan reversion and its defense implications. There was, for example, rather contradictory speculation that a "secret deal" involved Japan in the defense of the Republic of Korea and that the United States was shifting its Asian policy of withdrawal because she feared the resurgence of militarism in Japan. Then came a spate of articles from Washington correspondents assessing the temper of

American attitudes toward Japan and focusing on the "rise-of-militarism" angle.

The Johnson testimony, which fixed attention on U.S. attitudes, also provoked considerable commentary on the Nixon Doctrine and its effect upon Japan and the security treaty. An article by the foreign affairs commentator, Kusumi Tadao, in the *Yomiuri* of 25 August was representative. Basing his opinions on the revelation of the secret hearings before the U.S. Foreign Relations Committee, Kusumi concluded that the Nixon Doctrine was "being enforced" against Japan. For the first time, America expected Japan to defend its interests outside its borders. In view of the determination of the United States to extricate herself from Asia, Kusumi contended that it was only natural for the Japanese to feel that the Americans would attempt to transform the Japan-U.S. security treaty into a security treaty for the whole of Asia. After reviewing reports on the magnitude and diversity of the anticipated U.S. withdrawal, which would remove most American forces "to Guam or east of Guam by 1975," leaving behind only military assistance advisory groups, Kusumi concluded that the success of the American withdrawal depended upon Japan. Of all America's Asian allies, Japan alone might play a leading role in the security and stability of the region. Even *Pravda,* he pointed out, had said that Japan should take greater interest in the peace of Asia than the United States and had advocated Japan's entry into collective security arrangements. Japan, on the other hand, Kusumi continued, viewed her role far differently. He maintained that the Japanese tend to eschew the principle of collective security; he argued that Japan realizes the grave effect it would have upon Asian security if Japanese troops were to be sent abroad. As long as U.S. troops were scattered throughout the Pacific region, the situation posed no problem for Japan but their withdrawal would mean restudy by Tokyo's planners. Fortunately, he went on, a Pacific area treaty organization is not the only course open. Although economic aid and technical assistance will not be enough in themselves, Japan can offer international cooperation for settling disputes, and can make positive contributions toward liquidating the causes of social upheaval and preventing political infiltration. Japan can also support U.N. efforts to prevent war. Kusumi concluded that there are many ways for Japan to play a positive role in Asia without resorting to military force, and ways for the Japanese to take action independently of the United States to establish an international

Asian nations in the seventies. Articles like Kusumi's, a direct result of the Johnson incident, were obviously intended to sharpen Japan's general awareness that a turning point in her strategic position in Asia had been reached, and that the time had come for difficult decisions now that the American presence which had so long sheltered Japan, often over bitter objections, was in the process of being withdrawn.

Nakasone's Visit to the United States

With the background of summer-long discussions on defense affairs, the news media welcomed the announcement that beginning 8 September 1970 Nakasone would visit Washington for a series of talks with American defense officials. The "qualitative change" which the press saw in the security treaty and the serious manner in which the United States was moving to carry out the promise of the Nixon Doctrine made Nakasone's visit seem an absolute necessity. However, recalling the director-general's tendency toward colorful phrasing and outspoken attitudes, the newspapers gratuitously took the opportunity to caution him about the limits of his charter. A *Nihon Keizai* editorial on 7 September warned Nakasone not to be "venturesome," and enjoined him to "convey the government's unified view of the basis of defense" (meaning stay away from personal opinions) and to emphasize firmly that Japan will remain a nonnuclear nation and that her defense power will be used exclusively for defensive purposes. *Yomiuri,* on that same day, noted that the relative position of Japan's defense power within the security treaty arrangement was rising rapidly, and that in view of the retrenchment under the Nixon Doctrine, American leaders must harbor latent ideas that Japan's defense power would occupy an even more important position in the future. Since neither a basic policy nor the Fourth Defense Buildup Plan had at that time been settled upon, Japan was cautioned against disadvantageous commitments to the U.S. The editors then reminded Nakasone of the serious anxiety in Japan over deepening Japanese-U.S. security ties.

On the following day, when the director-general was to arrive in Washington. *Mainichi* urged discretion upon him, observing that relations between the two countries were in a "fluid" state and that the U.S., in an apparent period of neo-isolationism, was reducing conventional forces and seeking a new image in Asia. At the same time, Japan groped toward an autonomous defense policy and a new international

31

system of cooperation for progress and peaceful coexistence among role. As a consequence each side was probing the other, the United States seeking to know what to expect from Japan and Japan anxious to learn when and by how much American forces in East Asia would be reduced. Thus Nakasone should use care to avoid exciting the "doves" in either country and arousing suspicion about renewed Japanese militarism.

At the end of the trip (20 September), the press agreed that Nakasone had done well; it gave broad coverage to his accomplishments, and credited the U.S. secretary of defense with a sympathetic and understanding attitude. Such thorny issues as the joint use of U.S. bases in Japan, the speedy turnover of the troublesome bases in densely populated areas, and an agreement on Okinawa reversion arrangements now seemed nearer solution. The press gave guarded approval to the U.S. agreement to hold ministerial-level meetings when necessary to smooth the working of the security treaty and to exchange views on defense problems. There had been misgivings about this Nakasone proposal before he left. The newspapers also perceived improvement in more than just problems of day-to-day working relations. They seemed to feel that the "delicate distrust" between the two countries had somewhat dissipated. They felt more sure of the U.S. commitment to defend Japan and less uneasy over neo-isolationism and the withdrawal features of the Nixon Doctrine. The talks dispelled the rumors that the United States was pushing for a Japan-led PATO and the press conceded that Nakasone had to some degree quelled Amercan fears of revived militarism. He had told the Americans that Japan would continue to maintain the security treaty on a semipermanent basis and that Japan's forces would provide only local defense, a modification of what he had been advocating before August. He assured the United States that Japan was not reviving militarism and that she would not seek a nuclear capability of her own. He had said the proper things and he had said them forthrightly.

Nakasone's trip, if not a triumph, gave evidence of solid accomplishment. Only one serious misstep marred it for the press. The director-general had been "indiscreet" enough to propose that America assist in building a facility in Japan to produce enriched uranium 235 for use as fuel in atomic-power generation plants. Nakasone's previous positions qualified him to discuss nuclear matters, but it seemed inappropriate for the civilian head of the nation's armed forces to broach such a subject when his main concern was to convince his hosts that Japan had no intention of manufacturing or possessing nuclear weapons. In point of fact, the implication in Nakasone's proposal was that Japan would finally ratify the nuclear nonproliferation treaty once her source of nuclear fuel for power plants was guaranteed through co-production arrangements. An editorial in *Nihon Keizai* on 23 September also saw a contradiction between Nakasone's assertion that it was not Japan's intention to alarm any of her neighbors and his promise for a strong defensive effort in the forthcoming fourth defense plan. *Nihon Keizai* appealed to the government to be sensitive to foreign fears of renewed militarism, to concentrate on economic problems and, with due consideration for the lessons learned from Nakasone's trip, to implement the defense plan in a way that would cause no uneasiness abroad.

The Defense White Paper

After a hiatus of about a month, during which the defense problem languished in the news, attention focused once again on the Defense Agency. On 20 October the government at last presented the nation with its first defense white paper, *The Defense of Japan* (see Appendix, Document 9). Editorial response and analytical comment in all news media were immediate and coverage was heavy. Commentators restrained their praise for the paper but evinced satisfaction that it had been published and that the public had at last been told about Japan's defense and where it stood today. Some of the conclusions of the white paper were above reproach, such as the reiteration of the three nonnuclear principles, the pledge to possess no "offensive weapons," and a restatement of the policy that no Japanese troops would ever be sent abroad. There appeared to be a sense of relief that autonomous defense had not taken precedence over the Japan-U.S. security treaty, although this battle had been won in August and confirmed in Washington in September by Nakasone himself—the man who earlier had seemed to seek reversal of that order of precedence. Some newspapers expressly approved the tone of the paper at least in part. The *Mainichi* on 21 October liked the low posture given the Self Defense Forces and the idea of placing defense among national political issues. The *Tokyo Shimbun,* that same day, approved the white paper as a "reasonable framework," laying the defense problem before the people in broad context; the *Sankei,* which had little else good to say about it, agreed.

Two major criticisms, closely linked, appeared in most commentaries: first, that no specific limit was placed on conventional defense power outside the general limitations on the Constitution and government policy, and second, that no definitive limit was placed on defense expenditure. *The Defense of Japan* broke the policy for defense expenditure out of its previous mold—that of tying it to a percentage of the gross national product—and anchored it in a harmonious balance with social security and educational expenditures. For most interpreters this meant a year-by-year increase in defense expense if the economy improved, although a few conceded that the formula also could be used to decrease military expenditure relative to other parts of the budget. The majority seemed to feel that the government should formulate a defense policy and then compile a budget to satisfy Japan's strategic needs. It seemed clear that the level of defense expenditure was regarded more in terms of budget balancing than in guaranteeing Japan's security. The major concerns seemed to be for the cost to Japan and for the opinion of foreign nations.

Several papers noted with dismay that a statement against conscription had been removed from the final draft before publication. Many editors complained of the "flat" nature of the paper, the lack of anything new, the apparent haste with which it was written, its use of high-flown wording, and its sermon-like quality; several likened it to a government or Defense Agency rebuttal to a Diet interpellation. At least two editors objected to a statement that "defensive" nuclear weapons (apparently meaning either ABMs or tactical nuclear weapons for use against invading forces) per se were not barred from Japan by the Constitution but, rather, by the government's long-held policy of the three nonnuclear principles.

In the daily press, however, there was surprisingly little editorial analysis or political commentary which explicitly followed JSP arguments against defense policy or the security treaty. Some apprehensive writers argued that on the basis of the logic of the white paper, which makes collective security and autonomous defense compatible and denies the possibility of an ABM for Japan, Japan should seek nuclear guarantees from the United States, the Soviet Union, and China. Instead of depending so heavily on the American nuclear umbrella and large appropriations for conventional arms, the nation should turn to diplomacy and good neighborly relations which have a "special meaning for the security of our country." According to this argument, since Japan—as the white paper asserts—will strive for improved social welfare and for world peace instead of becoming a military great power, the achievement of security through multilateral guarantees or through dependence upon the United Nations would become more important than ever. This policy would refute allegations of a revival of militarism.[5]

Such arguments do not depend upon the Leninist thesis of imperialism as the highest stage of capitalism, the JSP argument for neutralism which makes the United States by definition an aggressor nation. However, an article by Professor Seki Hiroharu of Tokyo University pointed this way. Seki chided the government for expecting the United States to defend Japan with her deterrent power, an echo of the Gallois thesis,[6] and explained that Taiwan, South Korea, and the United States pursued "offensive strategies" while Japan held to a defensive strategy. Japan, he continued, will not have ICBMs or other offensive weapons, but the United States does, thereby posing a constant threat to China. With China's acquisition of the ICBM by the mid-seventies, tension would be bound to increase. Skirmishes in Taiwan could trigger a U.S. attack upon China, and, he intimated darkly, Japan, having made common cause with a nation on the strategic offensive, would be involved. As a consequence, the white paper statement that the security treaty would be effective in preventing the outbreak of armed conflict in East Asia and would contribute to Japan's security is in error.[7]

Other editorials and articles disagreed with specific statements of the white paper or saw contradictions within its pages. Some critics questioned the white paper's argument that diplomacy backed by military force is necessarily more effective, while others took exception to the white paper's emphasis on the threat of indirect aggression. They also noted that the white paper opposed Japan's becoming a big military power, yet cited as examples Sweden and Switzerland, both

---

[5] This section is based upon articles from the following newspapers: *Asahi Shimbun,* 20 and 23 October 1970; *Mainichi Shimbun,* 20, 21, and 23 October 1970; *Nihon Keizai Shimbun,* 21, 22, and 23 October 1970; *Sankei Shimbun,* 20, 21, and 23 October 1970; *Tokyo Shimbun,* 21, 22, and 24 October 1970; and *Yomiuri Shimbun,* 21 and 22 October 1970.
[6] This term is borrowed from French General Gallois, whose formulation provided De Gaulle with a rationale for France's nuclear armament.
[7] Seki Hiroharu, "Moot Points of Defense White Paper Criticized," *Yomiuri Shimbun,* 21 October 1970.

of which maintain their neutrality by large expenditures on conventional arms.

The sharp press reaction to *The Defense of Japan* was a response to an unfamiliar set of circumstances which created uneasiness not only in the press but in the nation at large. For the first time in their own words the press recognized that Japan was now exposed to the full impact of world politics. Defense in the larger sense had been an American problem. The Nixon Doctrine created new security burdens for Japan whether the country liked it or not. As *Sankei* pointed out on 21 October 1970, past debates about defense had been in the language of ideology, not reality. Japan must now abandon her policy of subservience in return for security. As a consequence of entering into the period of automatic continuation of the security treaty and of the application of the Nixon Doctrine, the country now possibly faced great increases in defense expenditures and increasing arguments for "autonomous defense." According to the *Nihon Keizai* of 21 October, the nation had to face the fact that the Fourth Defense Buildup Plan was already causing fear of militarism among friendly, as well as not so friendly, neighboring nations. *Asahi* (20 October) saw the whole dilemma of defense as the outgrowth of two conflicting systems, the Japan-U.S. security treaty system and the Peace Constitution. Their editors might have added that both were made in the U.S. The *Mainichi* (21 October 1970) posed the pertinent question—which, it commented, the white paper did not answer—as to how a joint Japanese-American defense of Japan could be successfully achieved if American forces were inevitably to be withdrawn from East Asia.

The Defense of Japan stimulated sober thought on the defense problems and raised some serious questions in Japanese minds. How is the Japan-U.S. "collective security" system to work? Will it tie Japan closer to the United States or will it mean Japanese commitments on the Asian continent? What are the practical aspects of an increase in Japan's will to defend itself? Does this mean conscription? Does it mean government-sponsored propaganda? What is war potential, and what is meant by the sustaining power of the Self Defense Forces? The Constitution expressly forbids war potential. If defenses are to be markedly increased, will the principle of civilian control be maintained? Can defense be integrated with the defense industry without producing a dangerous military-industrial complex? Such troublesome questions found no answer in the white paper. Warnings naturally followed. The policy-making process in defense matters should not contradict stated ideals. Civilian control should not mean control by Defense Agency bureaucrats. Safeguards should be established to prevent the return of militarism through a back door.

Nakasone had succeeded in making public the Defense Agency's first white paper. In so doing he appeared to compromise his earlier goals, but it is possible that they were merely trial balloons. If they were, the answer to them was definitive. The basic defense policy was not changed; the security treaty still took precedence over autonomous defense. In fact, when *Asahai* (20 October) compared the manuscript of an unpublished defense white paper of September 1969 with the published 1970 version, the earlier one, prepared when Arita Kiichi was director-general, rejected a policy of nonaligned neutrality, elevated autonomous defense over the security treaty, and laid stress on indirect aggression, indicating that Nakasone's defense program did not after all originate with him but had been the brainchild of Defense Agency officials.

Press Reaction to the Fourth Defense Buildup Plan

On the day following the release of the defense white paper, the Defense Agency officially announced the original draft of the Fourth Defense Buildup Plan (21 October 1970). Like the Third Defense Buildup Plan, it was to run for five years, beginning when the third ended after Japan's fiscal year 1971 (ending 31 March 1972). The plan's goal was to improve overall defense power in order to repel effectively any local aggression using conventional weapons. It provides the means to cope with direct or indirect aggression rapidly and flexibly. Its implementation would give the Ground Self Defense Force greater firepower and mobility, the Maritime Self Defense Force greater capability for sea and air defense, and the Air Self Defense Force a more advanced fighter aircraft for air defense of the homeland.

The draft plan, coming as it did on the heels of the defense white paper, invited the press to comment on it as the concrete embodiment of the basic policy in the white paper. Most press comment on the defense plan was unfavorable; the cost, estimated at that time to be 5.5 trillion yen, was the greatest single objection, but several other important points were raised. As might be expected, the defense-minded *Tokyo Shimbun* (23 October 1970) gave the most favorable response among the large dailies. Its editors did not balk at the cost, pointing out that under the plan Japan would still rank only eighteenth among the nations of the world in per capita defense expenditure. But they cautioned the government to study carefully and obtain popular understanding on the following five points:

(1) The fluidity of the world situation demands constant analysis of hypothetical emergency possibilities, and although such judgments are politically sensitive, they are necessary to ensure security; the government will, however, be wise not to inflate them out of proportion for the sake of increasing defense expenditure.

(2) The government must make the defense plan compatible with the security treaty. It will be necessary to discuss sharing missions with the United States.

(3) The Self Defense Forces must use manpower sparingly. An SDF of smaller size, but higher quality, may be the solution.

(4) There is the problem of a military-industrial complex, and it must be remembered that if private industry does not provide required material there may be a tendency to turn to SDF arsenals.

(5) It is absolutely necessary to maintain strong civilian control.

This was a very difficult list indeed. All previous public discussion of hypothetical enemies of Japan-U.S. combined planning had aroused strong feelings in opposition political circles and equally serious criticism in the press. The *Tokyo Shimbun* reminded its readers that in the 1960s the SDF had suffered a chronic shortage of quality enlistees; it warned that many Japanese foresaw a powerful, emerging military-industrial complex, even though there was no anticipation of government-run arsenals. The paper concluded that even a favorable disposition toward the plan did not make acceptance of its execution a foregone conclusion.[8]

Mainichi (23 October) took an even more equivocal stance. The editors pointed out that under the plan per capita expenditure was to double, and that the plan would reverse the downward trend of the ratio of defense expenditure to the gross national product, pushing it back up toward 1 percent. This matter required popular and Diet consideration. But *Mainichi* admitted that the need for a re-evaluation of defense

---

[8] *Tokyo Shimbun,* 22 and 24 October, 1970. Other newspapers consulted include: *Asahi Shimbun,* 23 October 1970; *Mainichi Shimbun,* 23 October 1970; *Nihon Keizai Shimbun,* 23 October 1970; *Sankei Shimbun,* 23 October 1970; and *Yomiuri Shimbun,* 22 October 1970.

problems was warranted because of the increase in Japan's economic power, the withdrawal of American strength from Asia, and the necessity for Japan to break away from the previous policy of "excessive protection." Since the white paper confirmed, however, that Japan faced no "imminent threat," there was no need for haste. After all, China and Russia were at loggerheads. The editors warned that since independence in defense was a goal, the trend of the changes as outlined in the defense plan was natural, but if, as some Finance Ministry officials were already warning, public welfare was to be slighted as a result, then the people would not understand. Japan must remember that defense expenditures were generally declining elsewhere in the world. (The editors did not explain the source of this information.)

In considering the plan, the editors found some disturbing questions. Can Japan reconcile the idea of air and naval superiority in the waters about Japan with the white paper statement that Japan would not possess weapons that give the threat of aggression to others? Can Japan have this kind of superiority without offensive weapons? Cannot the F-4 Phantom be an offensive weapon? Since, they concluded, offense or defense is not inherent in the nature of weapons themselves, defense cannot be gained through individual weapons but through a total system of equipment, strategy, and direction of security policy. The Diet was advised to focus on this when considering the plan.

Nihon Keizai (23 October 1970) represented an even more unfavorable view. Their editors' first complaint had to do with cost: "Since this plan soaks up an estimated .92 percent of the gross national product, is this not a high price to pay for conventional weapons which will rank Japan seventh in the world in armaments?" Then, rather curiously, since the plan is specific and finite as to what SDF will receive, they charged that the plan "has no brakes" and that the maximum defense limit was not made clear. They asked why offensive power was to be increased with the addition of Phantom jets, missile ships, helicopter carriers, and airborne mobility for the Ground SDF. For all the slogans about mechanization and modernization there was no plan for coordination with defense industry. Business must be careful not to invite charges of militarism by inappropriate remarks. Protection of this environment, not an armament plan, was the best guarantee of security. In sum, they charged that the plan would cause a conflict in public opinion, a renewal of the constitutional debate, and international uneasiness over Japanese militarism.

The most critical viewpoint was expressed by *Asahi* in an editorial on 23 October. That influential newspaper characterized the plan as a vivid example of how Japan might become a military great power as the reformists had warned. "Why do we, who profess to be defensive, need the world's seventh greatest military strength? Our Peace Constitution says we will have no war potential. Let us return to the Constitution in its original form." Japan, the editorial continued, should "hold nationwide discussions on the way to insure the security of our country and on the limitations of self-defense power." This should be done before arguing over the propriety of individual targets for the consolidation of defense power.

But having said this, *Asahi,* too, tacitly accepted the current structure of the SDF by granting that better pay and weapons procurement for the SDF were legitimate expenditures. Their objections were to the magnitude of the expense (1.9 times as large for the Ground SDF, 2.3 times for the Maritime SDF and 2.8 times for the Air SDF) and to the danger of swelling the coffers of industry so that a military-industrial complex would arise. They were concerned also about the dual nature of the new weapons which made offensive ones indistinguishable from defensive ones. Sato had told the world in his U.N. General Assembly speech that Japan would not spend great amounts for military purposes, but in the eyes of many the Fourth Defense Buildup Plan belied his statement.

On 22 October the *Yomiuri* published the critical reactions of the opposition parties to the Fourth Defense Buildup Plan. The various party statements contained little that was new. The JSP, in keeping with its allegation that Japan was going to return to militarism (a stance virtually indistinguishable from that of Asian Communist powers), charged that the plan exceeded the limits of defense, that the expenditures were to be "huge" and that the plan, by falling in line with the Japan-U.S. joint communiqué of November 1969, aimed at extending Japanese power to Korea and Taiwan. To the JSP, the plan increased apprehensions in Asia and signaled the beginning of militarization on a large scale by creating defense senior high schools and fostering domestic weapons production at the behest of business circles, thus strengthening the military-industrial complex. The *Komeito* took a somewhat more moderate tone, alleging that the plan opened the way to revision of the Constitution and would make Japan a big military power. Demanding suspension of the plan, that party advocated a peace plan to restore relations with China and peace without armament. The mild statement of the DSP concentrated on the plan's ambiguity. How would the people's consent be obtained; how would resources be allocated? If autonomous defense was to be reality, the choice of the weapons in the plan was wrong. Concentrating on the government's subservience to the exigencies of American "aggressive, imperialist strategy in East Asia," the JCP accused the government of planning to turn the SDF into an instrument for aggressive local war in Asia. The plan increased Japan's capability for military aggression through ground and naval operations outside the country and for bombing other nations. As expected, each party had blasted the plan from behind the ramparts of its own *Weltanschauung*.

3

The Alleged Revival of Japanese Militarism

A Revival of Japanese Militarism?

Charges made outside Japan about a revival of Japanese militarism have inevitably affected Japanese attitudes toward rearmament. Countries which portrayed Japan's qualitatively improved defense establishment as a threat based their conclusion on Japanese prewar military history and the present world position of Japan's economy. Peking's propaganda in 1970 and 1971 played this theme with continuing and increasing stridency, varying the expression but leaving no doubt about the message. Moscow also conjured up a dangerous return to the old-time Japanese military power but pursued the line with overtones different from those used by the Chinese. Southeast Asians have long complained of alleged Japanese economic domination—through denuding these nations of their raw materials and flooding them with exports—and have foreseen a future renascence of Japanese militarism. Americans have also warned of the prospects that Japan will again acquire threatening military power.[1] Opposition parties within Japan, which reject the Self Defense Forces and try in every way to obstruct enactment of higher defense budgets, have attempted to win political capital by exploiting the revival-of-militarism charge. That all of this publicity, whether of foreign or domestic origin, has influenced popular attitudes was indicated by public opinion polls which showed a considerable

---

[1] See Albert Axelbank, *Black Star Over Japan* (New York: Farrar, Straus and Giroux, Inc., 1972), and U.S. Congress, House of Representatives, Committee on Foreign Affairs, *Report of Special Study Mission to Asia*, 22 April 1970.

percentage of Japanese citizens who believed that militarism was indeed being revived.

Attitudes in Foreign Countries

China. Chinese accusations that Japan was reviving militarism are not new. They were made against Prime Minister Kishi in the years 1958-1960. They became a Peking propaganda theme, however, in 1970, after Premier Chou En-lai journeyed to Pyongyang, the capital of North Korea, for meetings with Premier Kim Il-sung. Chou made several statements in Pyongyang about Japanese militarism, each one with a slightly different nuance. Upon arrival at the airport on 5 April, Chou spoke of Japanese reactionaries who, as the vanguard of American imperialism, were "increasingly reviving militarism." At a welcome banquet the same evening, he denounced the Sato regime as the most reactionary and most tainted with aggression of any Japanese government since the Second World War, a regime which was "planning to follow the old road of Japanese militarism, trying again to reconstruct the old illusion of a Greater East Asia Co-Prosperity Sphere." By 7 April, Chou had concluded that Japanese militarism was no longer merely a danger, but had become a reality. At the end of the conference the two prime ministers signed a communiqué which devoted nine paragraphs to Japanese militarism. The first one read:

> The two sides vehemently condemned Japanese militarism which, revived again as a dangerous force of aggression in Asia under the active patronage of U.S. imperialism, is embarking on the road of open aggression against the Asian people with a delusion to realize the old broken dream of "Greater East Asia Co-Prosperity Sphere" with the backing of U.S. imperialism and in conspiracy and collusion with it.[2]

Similarly, Japanese and Chinese delegates to trade conferences in Peking have vigorously condemned Japanese militarism. Representatives of certain "friendly firms" and their Chinese counterparts stated categorically in a communiqué issued 14 April 1970 that "militarism had revived" in Japan.[3] Five days later, another Sino-Japanese joint

---

[2] *Pyongyang Times* (Pyongyang, Democratic People's Republic of North Korea), no. 14 (272), 13 April 1970, p. 11.
[3] For the text see "Friendly Firms Communiqué," New China News Agency (Peking), 15 April 1970.

communiqué, issued following the annual negotiations on the so-called Memorandum Trade Agreement in which the Japanese participants were members of the governing Liberal Democratic Party, mentioned, at Chinese insistence, the revival of Japanese militarism.[4] The 1971 trade communiqué, signed on 1 March, declared that Japanese reactionaries were colluding with American imperialists to use Japan as a base for aggression in Asia; this confirmed "that the revival of Japanese militarism had already become a reality." The Japanese signatories of the document expressed, on their part, determination to fight against and stop this revival of militarism.

Chinese propaganda organs interpreted numerous events in Japan as signs of revived militarism. When the defense white paper was issued on 1 October 1970, the Chinese professed alarm, seeing in it a plan for war and aggression instead of a policy for legitimate defense. They described the spectacular suicide of Mishima Yukio on 25 November of the same year as a danger signal portending a rise in the power of the rightists and their eventual remilitarization of the country. Peking Radio connected Mishima's act with dark plots of the Sato government, terming the incident "ironclad evidence of the revival of militarism by the Sato government." Announcements of figures for the Fourth Defense Buildup Plan evoked signals from Peking's press and radio that here was a blueprint for building militarism, "obviously aimed," as the *Peking Review* described it, "at stepping up expansion abroad and preparing for an aggressive war . . . nothing but a refurbishing of the so-called 'self-existence, self-defense' advocated by Hideki Tojo in the past." [5]

By far the clearest and most dispassionate Chinese case for the revival of Japanese militarism was made by Premier Chou En-lai in his lengthy interview with *New York Times* vice president and columnist James Reston on 5 August 1971. Chou made several points. His first was that the United States had strengthened the Japanese reactionaries in the postwar period and that the great economic expansion of Japan would inevitably induce the growth of militarism. Secondly, Chou argued that the United States had promoted such growth by prolonging indefinitely its security treaty with Japan. Reston countered by suggesting that without the pact, Japan's incentive to "go nuclear"

---

[4] For the text see New China News Agency, 19 April 1970.
[5] *Peking Review*, 25 June 1971, p. 2.

would increase. Chou called this a "forced argument" but was unconvincing in his attempt to refute it. Cataloging Japan's capacities for producing missiles, bombers, and nuclear weapons, Chou contended that Japan could not be prevented from making nuclear weapons "merely by the treaty." Third, he propounded his thesis that "economic expansion is bound to bring about military expansion," citing Japanese films on military themes, the Mishima suicide, and the mid-air collision of a Japanese fighter and a civilian airliner (supposedly proving unrestricted military monopoly of air space), to bolster his conclusion that the Japanese were restoring militarism. A fourth reason for Chou En-lai's fear of a remilitarized Japan was the Chinese memory of Japanese aggression: "You know we suffered a long time, for fifty years." A final and perhaps even more serious consideration for Chou was the Nixon Doctrine which aimed, in his view, to arm America's "partners," the principal one of which was Japan.[6]

Reston himself summed up Chou's attitude toward Japan in a separate article written from Peking in the course of which he characterized the showing to him of Japanese war movies as a symbol of an "anxiety amounting almost to an aberration." He noted that "the combination of past experience with Japan, plus the Nixon Doctrine of 'sharing' the defense of East Asia with Japan, plus Japan's economic and military development all add up here to one more official nightmare, and the Japanese movies in this context seem to the Chinese to help prove their point."[7]

Notably Chou En-lai did not say to Reston, as he had declared in Pyongyang the year before, that militarism *had already revived* in Japan. Instead, he predicted that "they are *bound to develop militarism,*" and advised, "When you oppose a danger, you should oppose it when it is only budding." This sounded less dogmatic than the words of the March communiqué, "the revival of Japanese militarism has already become a reality."

Two months before the Reston interview, the *Peking Review* had used the present tense to describe "the ambition of reviving Japanese militarism," and in October when a group of multi-party Diet representatives visited Peking, the Chinese termed the revival of Japanese militarism a *threat* to the peoples of Asia but refrained from calling

---

[6] *Asahi Evening News,* 23 August 1971.
[7] Ibid., 14 August 1971.

it a *reality*. Later in the same month, 28 October, Chou En-lai conversed at length with the managing director of the Tokyo *Asahi Shimbun* and made no mention of militarism.[8] In November the Chinese premier met a group of Japanese industrial and financial leaders. In tailoring his arguments to fit the interests and backgrounds of his listeners, he described the "distorted" development of the Japanese economy as indicated by its imbalances (1) in foreign exchange (preponderance of dollars and pounds instead of gold), (2) between resources and transportation, (3) between cities and rural areas, and (4) with respect to public nuisances in cities and to the general worsening of environmental conditions. Chou was convinced that to overcome such critical problems Japan would move toward expansion overseas which would in turn lead to Japanese domination of other nations and to the development of militarism. He concluded that whether the Japanese government desired militarism or not, and in spite of the fact that a great majority of the Japanese people opposed militarism, "there is possibility that the present form of the development of the Japanese economy will turn into militarism." [9]

These declarations differed from the categorical statements of 1970 and early 1971. Chinese leaders may have concluded that their propaganda had been overdone and that, in view of the impending visit of President Nixon and its possible influence in Japan, some toning down would be advisable. Perhaps they saw that with the Sato regime inevitably nearing an end, opportunities for more direct and profitable influence in Tokyo might now be worth seeking actively, and that to be successful, somewhat more tactful references to the likelihood of a Japanese revival of militarism would be wise. Chinese propaganda organs did not, however, remove militarism completely from their armory. On the eve of the President's arrival in Peking the *Hsinhua* News Agency warned that President Nixon and Defense Secretary Laird were enlisting "the services of Japanese militarism" to commit aggression in Asia by modernizing Japan's armed forces.[10]

Several factors explain the Chinese campaign against Japanese militarism. One must be the place of Japan in China's world view. To the present leaders of China, who themselves experienced the war and occupation brought to China by the Japanese in the 1930s, it

---

[8] *Asahi Shimbun,* 6 November 1971.
[9] See *Nihon Keizai Shimbun,* 19 November 1971.
[10] See *New York Times,* 19 February 1973.

47

must be difficult to believe that the expansionist urge is entirely dead. Chou En-lai seemed convinced that a huge economic power with Japan's history must inevitably become a military power. Regardless of whether this was genuine conviction or propaganda tactics, Chou had come full circle when in 1973, after diplomatic relations had opened with Japan, he admitted the need for Japan to possess its own armed forces and to continue the security treaty with the United States.[11]

Prime Minister Sato and his "reactionary clique" had been early named as one of the "four enemies" of China, and Chou En-lai publicly rejected a visit by Sato to Peking. The Chinese, sensing correctly the "China mood" in Japan and the popularity of any steps toward normalization of Chinese-Japanese relations, were happy to encourage those Japanese political forces fighting the LDP and flaunting the menace of nascent militarism before the public. Chou may have had no illusions about imminent political upheaval in Japan but he sought to encourage opponents of the ruling group in any way he could. At the same time, he showed a readiness—even eagerness—to be more amenable to Sato's successor. As the four-term prime minister's stay in office neared its end, the charges of revival of militarism almost disappeared from Chinese media and opportunities for improved relations clearly lay ahead.

For the Chinese one of the most compelling considerations in any policy relating to Japan is always its effect on China's arch rival, the Soviet Union. China was in the favored position with regard to Japan, not only because Japan's desire to improve relations with the People's Republic was stronger than ever before, but because the Chinese image in Japan was far brighter than that of the Soviet Union. Although at bitter odds with the Japanese Communist Party, the Chinese have enjoyed good relations with other parties, including certain groups within the LDP, all of whom vied with each other in sending delegations to Peking. Furthermore, China has not suffered a handicap of the kind of territorial issue which, in the case of the Russians, has reduced their popularity among the Japanese and so far has been the obstacle to a peace treaty between the two countries.

The Chinese enjoy an additional advantage. Many Japanese still feel guilt for the depredations of their soldiery in China and sense that

---

[11] Interview between Premier Chou En-lai and LDP Dietman Kimura Takeo. See *Asahi Shimbun* (evening edition), 18 January 1973.

they owe restitution to their neighbors on the mainland.[12] The Chinese may conclude that such guilt feelings make the Japanese more susceptible to warnings over reviving militarism sounded in Peking and cause them to react more seriously than otherwise would be the case.

The Soviet Union. Leonid Brezhnev, secretary-general of the Soviet Communist Party reported to the Twenty-fourth Party Congress, convened in Moscow on 30 March 1971, that "forces of war and aggression exist in Japan. They are militarists who, in defiance of the constitution which has renounced war for good, are again trying to push the nation toward the path to territorial expansion and aggression." In Soviet eyes, "the path to territorial expansion" is Japan's claim to certain islands in the Kurile chain, and this claim, coupled with a specter of reviving militarism, conjured up the vision of a resurgent, threatening Japan. For some time this theme characterized Moscow's propaganda, which found vestiges of old-time right-wing warmongering still active in Japan, as evidenced by war films, Mishima's suicide, and campaigns to revise the Constitution. The main culprit who cunningly prods the Japanese to retrace their path of infamy, however, is always the United States. The Soviet line was that the Americans were forcing the Japanese to rearm rapidly, to take over American military responsibilities in Asia, to defend American military bases in Okinawa, to buy weapons "made-in-U.S.A.," and to forge a multilateral, militaristic bloc of Asian nations.

While Moscow competed with Peking to raise the alarm over Japanese militarism, the two capitals did not send out the same messages. The Soviets condemned a process which could still be diverted, while the Chinese, at least in the beginning, spoke of accomplished fact. Chou worried about the Nixon Doctrine and the Japanese-American security treaty and their influence on Japanese militarism, but the Russians made more of American complicity in the rearmament of Japan. Soviet radio and newspaper commentators saw American monopolists as villains who were pushing Japan toward dangerous, aggressive adventures.

The Soviets interpreted higher Japanese defense budgets as signals of a booming military production, with the major monopolies (Mitsui, Mitsubishi, and Sumitomo) forming an unholy alliance with the Penta-

---

[12] See Edwin O. Reischauer, *Japan: The Story of a Nation* (New York: Knopf, 1970), p. 268, for a discussion of the Japanese "guilt complex."

gon-like power of the Defense Agency, a new collusion between *gumbatsu* (military) and *zaibatsu* (industrial monopolies). Moscow's media characterized the Fourth Defense Buildup Plan as a far-reaching design of Japan's ruling circles and monopoly capital to expand military potential in spite of the Constitution. *Izvestiya* warned of the "dangerous alliance . . . between the armament industry monopolies of Japan and the United States" and interpreted Japan's arms production as directed toward "the goal of re-creating a strong Japanese army and establishing the dominance of Japanese monopoly capital in the area of Southeast Asia and the Pacific Ocean."[13]

President Nixon's State of the World Message inspired Soviet propagandists to discover in the Nixon Doctrine a plot to get Japan to assume American military responsibilities in Asia. Vladimir Yakovlev, Radio Moscow commentator, affirmed that "the United States expects to make Japan take over part of its military and financial burden in the suppression of the national liberation movements in Asia." Yakovlev read into the President's message "an open call" on Japan to establish a regional bloc, military in nature, to include "puppet troops armed by Japan" (South Vietnam, Cambodia, and Laos), dependent upon Japan and under a military treaty with Japan by which these "puppet regimes . . . and troops will work for Japanese intentions."[14]

The visit to Japan of Secretary of Defense Laird in July 1971 set off a spate of Soviet commentaries on the theme of American promotion of Japanese militarism. The Soviets described the purposes of the trip as "to consolidate the American-Japanese military alliance," to establish a multilateral defense system in the Far East under American control, and to push Tokyo on the path of further militarization. Many saw Laird as encouraging Japanese militarism for American purposes, trying to "palm off" on Japan part of America's policing functions in Asia.

The treaty for the return to Japan of the administrative rights over Okinawa became in Soviet eyes an American scheme to force Japan to militarize more quickly and to defend American military bases and interests in the Ryukyu Islands. Moscow predicted that after Okinawan reversion, American forces would ignore the restrictions stipulated by the security treaty (which would then apply to Okinawa)

---

[13] *Izvestiya* (Moscow), 26 February 1971.
[14] Radio Moscow, 10 March 1971.

and would "continue to act as masters." In December 1971, Moscow Radio proclaimed that "Okinawa reversion hides Japanese militarization"; it warned that the United States was trying "to make Japan play a more concrete military role in Asia and shoulder part of the burden of the so-called defense of Asia." The forthcoming January meetings between Prime Minister Sato and President Nixon were interpreted as based on the goal of strengthening military ties between Washington and Tokyo and achieving the rapid militarization of Japan.

The special interests of the Soviet Union—particularly Japanese claims to the Soviet-held Kurile Islands—were revealed in their sensitivity toward Japanese air and naval activities in areas near Soviet territory and toward publicity for Japanese territorial demands. *Red Star* complained that in 1970 Japanese military aircraft had flown twenty-six "premeditated overflights" over Soviet merchant and fishing ships, more than three times the number of such incidents in 1969. Such actions were seen as evidence of "the increasingly intensive militarization of Japan and the propagation of revanchist ideas." These flights and "the policy of further militarization of the country are links in a single chain."[15] Russian radio broadcasts depicted the accidental firing on a Soviet ship by a Japanese air defense plane which occurred in March as a "sign of Japanese militarism." In the same month a *Pravda* correspondent linked posters at the annual Hokkaido snow festival calling for return of the northern islands with appeals for new recruits for the armed forces and with "the Japanese militarists."[16] In June 1971, Soviet propaganda organs scored joint maneuvers by American and Japanese naval forces as designed to "create tensions" and as "contrary to the desires of the people."

Moscow press and radio have frequently warned of the threat to Southeast Asia of Japanese economic and military expansion. Elaborating on a possibility which the Japanese themselves have discussed, TASS predicted on 5 March 1971 that Japan's expanding economic interests would inspire deployment of Japanese military forces in Southeast Asia for the protection of these interests. At the same time, Moscow Radio accused several leading Japanese industrialists and the director-general of the Defense Agency of "calling in chorus for stationing troops in Southeast Asia." A radio commentator denounced Japanese cooperation with American aggression aimed at

---

[15] *Red Star* (Moscow), 10 February 1971.
[16] *Pravda* (Moscow), 29 March 1971.

Asian nations which, combined with Japan's lust for territorial expansion, could only "lead toward repeating its tragedy of the past."[17] On 13 May 1971 an *Izvestiya* writer pictured in gloomy terms a Japan striving to impose economic hegemony in Southeast Asia. The Asian and Pacific Council was seen as an organization being utilized by Japan to further not only economic, but also military goals in Asia.

In spite of the intensity of the Soviet barrage against Japanese militarism, the main charges were that militarism was in the process of reviving. While Soviet propagandists did speak of the Japanese following the path to *further* militarization, they chiefly claimed that the new defense plan "would revive" militarism or "serves military interests" or "augurs military expansion." Statements frequently appeared suggesting that "the Japanese public is fully resolved to prevent its country from slipping down the path of new militaristic adventures." Finally, Secretary-General Brezhnev's warning about the revival of Japanese militarism should be placed in the context of his reference at the Twenty-fourth Party Congress to the Soviet government's policy to promise good relations with Japan on a basis of reciprocity and neighborly amity.

Although there was much similarity between the content of Chinese and Soviet propaganda on the subject of a revival of Japanese militarism, the particular interests of each country determined the emphasis and nuances of that propaganda. Several factors motivated the Soviets. The Soviet Union, while sharing with China a geographical position as neighbor to Japan, must also look upon Japan as a potential threat for the future. Consequently some degree of genuine apprehension over the rapid remilitarization of a former enemy must be harbored by the Kremlin leaders. They doubtless still see the Kurile chain as important to Soviet defense, as Stalin so persuasively argued to President Roosevelt at Yalta in 1945. At the same time, the Russians may take a somewhat sophisticated view of contemporary Japan in recognition of the frailty of the contention that Japanese militarism has already revived or is indeed a serious threat in the forseeable future.

In Soviet calculations the Chinese-Japanese equation is doubtless of priority concern. A major tenet of Soviet foreign policy must be to prevent these two Asian powers from close collaboration. At the same time that Moscow has tried to woo Japan away from China, she has

---

[17] Moscow Radio, 6 March 1971.

condemned the Japanese trend toward militarism, blaming it, however, not on the Japanese people but largely on the United States.

In the later months of 1971 the propaganda about militarism in Japan tapered off, to pave the way for Foreign Minister Gromyko's January visit to Tokyo. The meetings were successful from the Japanese point of view principally because Gromyko did not insist, as all Soviet representatives had invariably done before, that the territorial issue was already settled; he agreed to negotiate a peace treaty "within the year." Gromyko took special pains at the end of the talks to state that while the Soviet Union had no objections to efforts by Japan and other nations to improve their relations with China, "we must ask them to take care not to impair their relations with the Soviet Union or the interests and security of the Soviet Union."[18]

The Japanese were hopeful that the Gromyko visit presaged more profitable economic relations with the Russians and, of more importance, a peace treaty which would resolve the long-standing problem of the northern islands. Nothing was apparently said in Tokyo about militarism nor did Gromyko mention the security treaty with the United States nor the consequent stationing of American forces in Japan, facts which had been cited in the past by Moscow as obstacles to a final treaty of peace. Foreign Minister Fukuda went out of his way to reassure Gromyko about militarism and about relations with China. He declared categorically that Japan would "absolutely not become a militarized nation nor a nuclear-holding nation" and noted that no clue had yet been found for the normalization of relations with China.

The United States. The United States, through General MacArthur, first brought into being a Japanese defense force, and close Japanese-American cooperation in defense matters continued in the post-occupation period. As a consequence American attitudes toward the rearmament of Japan have carried great weight. American policy has encouraged the development of efficient Japanese self-defense forces, including efforts to persuade the Japanese government to increase defense budgets and, more particularly and more recently, to buy American military equipment. Before he was elected President, Richard M. Nixon publicly expressed the opinion that Japan should amend the

---

[18] *Nihon Keizai Shimbun,* 28 January 1972, and *New York Times,* 29 January 1972.

"no-war" article of her Constitution and assume greater defense responsibilities in East Asia.[19] It has never been United States policy, however, to take an official position for or against amendment of the Japanese Constitution and in recent years American official statements have paid respect to Japan's constitutional limitations. The President's 1970 report to the Congress, *U.S. Foreign Policy for the 1970s: A New Strategy for Peace,* assured the Japanese that "we shall not ask Japan to assume responsibilities inconsistent with the deeply felt concerns of its people" (see Appendix, Document 8). With respect to nuclear weapons, American policy was embodied in the nuclear nonproliferation treaty which the United States urged Japan to sign and ratify.[20]

In April 1970 the Japanese were surprised by the publication in Washington of a report made to the House Foreign Affairs Committee by Representatives Lester L. Wolff and J. Herbert Burke who had visited Asia. Their "Study Mission" report concluded that Japan was turning toward a "new militarism":

> There is a strong effort under way by some groups in Japan toward rearmament and a seeming return to the old "Greater East Asia Co-prosperity Sphere." The Study Mission was concerned with the increased emphasis by some on enlarging Japan's military prowess, even though it already supports the sixth [sic] largest military establishment in the world. . . .
> Placing this aspect of our report in perspective, the Study Mission evidences concern over Japan's emphasis on the new militarism. There seems to be a readiness to commit a substantial portion of Japan's vast wealth to the reestablishment of a major international military force. This involves increased spending, a much greater definition of her area of defense, nuclear capability, and a clear determination to be a military power on a scale not contemplated since World War II.[21]

The congressional report drew little attention in the United States but became front-page news in Japan. The Japanese media indicated confusion over inconsistent American attitudes toward Japan. On the one hand, Americans were blaming the Japanese for taking a "free

---

[19] Richard M. Nixon, "Asia After Viet Nam," *Foreign Affairs,* vol. 46, no. 1 (October 1967), p. 120.
[20] Japan signed the treaty on 3 February 1970 but had not ratified it as of May 1973.
[21] U.S. Congress, House of Representatives, *Report of Special Study Mission to Asia.*

ride" by spending too little on defense, and on the other, American lawmakers were upbraiding them for creating a "new militarism." The propaganda line of Peking and Moscow was familiar to Japanese but such charges from Washington, especially by members of Congress, could be expected to disconcert many Japanese newspaper readers and television viewers.[22]

In addition to conclusions which could be drawn from the congressional report, some Japanese, in spite of Washington's declarations to the contrary, harbored impressions that the American government would in fact be happy if Japan were to assume military obligations in Asia. The furor which arose in Tokyo in the summer of 1971 at the time of Defense Secretary Laird's visit reinforced these feelings. After a background press briefing, correspondents reported that the United States would not object to a Japanese decision to produce nuclear weapons. Repeated denials did not remove the impression left in the Japanese public mind. At the same time, frequent references by Americans to Japan's "free ride" in obtaining a security guarantee at American expense fostered the impression of a United States defending Asia, while Japan, relieved of any responsibility for military effort, grew rich.

American policy, as communicated publicly by the President, officials in the Department of State, and in the American embassy in Tokyo, however, was consistent.[23] The United States supported the continuation of the security treaty, as confirmed in repeated meetings between the prime minister and the President, and the United States never suggested that Japan produce or possess nuclear weapons. On the contrary, U.S. officials urged Japan to sign the nuclear nonproliferation treaty. American recognition of Japanese nuclear sensitivities found expression in the Sato-Nixon joint communiqué of November 1969 and again in the San Clemente joint statement of January 1972, the latter as a result of strong Japanese requests for assurances that nuclear weapons would be removed from Okinawa. Yet after reports

---

[22] One noted American authority on Asia has said with regard to American policy toward Japanese security, "Perhaps the most important fact is that to the Japanese, the United States has seemed ambivalent and unclear with respect to Japanese security policies, and more important, with respect to the broad course desirable for Japanese foreign policy." Robert Scalapino, *American-Japanese Relations in a Changing Era* (New York: Library Press, 1972), p. 109.

[23] The President's foreign policy report for 1973 emphasized Japan's "important steps toward self-reliance and improved capacity for conventional defense." See Appendix, Document 15.

of the Laird briefings and despite the denials which ensued, the Japanese press reflected uncertainty. Understandably disturbing were reports of revelations in the United States, of background briefings, and of statements by American military officials which seemed to hint that Japan might develop nuclear weapons with American blessing or that if Japanese-American relations deteriorated, Japan would be lured into the arms of the Soviet Union or Communist China. The Japanese also discovered that, in sharp conflict to the official policy statements, the views of the two congressmen were shared by other Americans. The *Yomiuri* newspaper asked Gallup to take a poll in the United States in the fall of 1971 to test American attitudes toward Japan. This poll showed that 67 percent of the American respondents felt that greater military strength for Japan would be harmful to the United States because Japan was untrustworthy.[24]

Thus, the message from the United States has not always seemed clear. Foreign opinion, especially American opinion, receives broad coverage in Japan, and American statements carry weight among the Japanese; consciously or unconsciously, Japanese attitudes are affected by them.

Political Parties

The theme of "reviving militarism" is, as we have seen, not unknown to the political parties opposing the Japanese government.

The Japan Communist Party, as one of Peking's proclaimed "four enemies," was accused by Premier Chou En-lai of encouraging the Sato government in its alleged pursuit of remilitarization. The JCP reacted angrily. The party's secretary-general, Miyamoto Kenji, retorted that so long as Article 9 survived and neither conscription nor the dispatch of military forces abroad was permitted, militarism had not yet revived. JCP spokesmen continued to warn, however, that militarism could be in the process of reviving and was a force dangerous for the future.

Other opposition parties echoed much of the Chinese line. The Socialists confirmed in a visit of their leaders to Peking that they accepted almost without reservation the Chinese position on Japanese militarism; the *Komeito* and DSP took a less militant line. For the

---

[24] *Yomiuri Shimbun,* 18 November 1971.

record, all four opposition parties publicly lamented the revival of militarism, but differed widely in their views as to the danger of its revival and the nature of its threat.

Those members of the LDP who made annual pilgrimages to Peking to negotiate the agreements on trade were generally sympathetic to the People's Republic of China and readily signed joint communiqués with the Chinese admitting the revival of Japanese militarism. These acts proved to Chou En-lai's satisfaction that "opposition elements" within Japan's ruling party agreed with his estimates of Japanese militarism. Whether the signers of these agreements believed in what they signed or were ready to compromise their convictions in the interest of China trade was debatable. In 1970 the party chastised its negotiators after their return from Peking; a majority statement regretted that the Chinese had failed to understand the "self-evident principle" that the "criticism and slander against the government of another nation"—as contained in the communiqué signed by the LDP representatives—was "an insult to the people of that country."[25] In 1971 the LDP membership did not bother to react to the March communiqué of that year. At the end of the year, however, the Party Disciplinary Committee created a national sensation by making an unprecedented decision in declaring ineligible for any party post Fujiyama Aiichiro, prominent LDP leader and a former foreign minister. The justification was Fujiyama's signing in Peking of a communiqué, issued after the visit of an interparliamentary delegation, which, among other criticisms of Japanese official policy, denounced the treaty between Japan and the Republic of China on Taiwan. The committee called Fujiyama's action an "imprudent and disgraceful act against the party." Fujiyama received strong support from within the party and enforcement of the decision was suspended.

Ohira Masayoshi, a former cabinet minister and at the time a leading candidate to succeed Sato Eisaku as prime minister, expressed an authoritative view in November 1971:

> Japan is a big economic power depending on peaceful markets in the world. In other words, world peace is essential for the existence of Japan. Japan, therefore, cannot become a military state. As for military strength sufficient to protect

---

[25] See *Nihon Keizai Shimbun,* 23 May 1970, for a discussion of the LDP statement which was issued on 28 April.

Japan's foreign trade, however much Japan might wish to build it up, such expansion would never be adequate nor would it be possible to carry on.[26]

Popular Attitudes

The Japanese man-in-the-street pays inordinate attention to comments made about him by foreigners. Foreign charges that the Japanese people were reviving militarism, so vigorously put forth by Peking, matched by Moscow, and echoed in Washington, therefore, were not taken lightly by the public. Popular reactions—except among the committed left—were mixed: resentment, incredulity, and bewilderment, and also serious soul-searching as to whether indeed the danger of a return to militarism might be more than just the nightmare of a ghost of the past. While defending their country against accusations which they felt to be unjust, those who communicated in the public media urged reflection and caution for the future.

An *Asahi* columnist wrote in August 1971:

> Ohira's opinion has not only been reflected in statements by other officials and defense specialists, who aver that another Seventh Fleet would be required to defend Japan's extended sea-lanes for trade, but Ohira's appointment as Foreign Minister in the Tanaka cabinet lends force to his views.
> While foreign concern seems to be exaggerated, it may be that the Japanese are too innocent or insensitive. Japan has a long way to go before militarism-oriented political and economic systems become a reality. But the Japanese, being nonchalant, cannot be counted on to work strongly against militarism when the situation develops seriously in that direction. We might as well take what foreigners say as a danger signal for such a future eventuality.[27]

Another leading newspaper, the *Mainichi,* rejected the proposition that Japan's economic expansion would lead to militarism, but nevertheless called for "self-reflection and "self-discipline" by Japanese business circles.

---

[26] *Jiyu Shimpo* (LDP official organ), 1 November 1971.
[27] *Asahi Evening News,* 14 August 1971.

On what grounds does China clamor against the "revival of Japanese militarism?" . . . our country is now tackling a "historical experiment" promoting economic advance into foreign countries in an atmosphere of peace to the last, without the backing of military force . . . . "economic expansion which will give rise to military expansion" cannot occur in our country where the peace constitution is fixed. However . . . stern reflection and self-discipline on the part of our country's business circles are necessary.[28]

The Japanese have been consistently testing their own attitudes toward the revival of militarism. Public opinion surveys on the subject have been frequent, especially during 1971. Some results are inconsistent and if one tries to draw general conclusions from a series of polls, contradictions among them become immediately evident. For example, a poll in December 1970 showed that 50 percent of the respondents believed that militarism had not "begun to revive"; 22 percent thought it had, and almost 30 percent replied "don't know." Almost a year later, in answer to a question which was phrased slightly differently, a total of 60 percent of those polled replied that either militarism *was reviving* (21 percent) or that its revival was *possible* (39 percent). In contrast to the 50 percent of 1970, only 28 percent believed militarism had *not revived*; 1 percent thought it had.

When the questions were rephrased to designate China as the originator of the militarism charges, the number of answers reflecting concern over possible revival of militarism went up. Japan's national broadcasting system (NHK) queried listeners in September 1971 about the "Chinese charges." The largest single percentage (23 percent) "understood Communist China's feeling but did not believe its position correct." More than 19 percent thought China "right to a certain degree" and 18.7 percent agreed that the revival of militarism was a danger for the future. Thus a combination of these two percentages representing an attitude of apprehension over a revival of Japanese militarism (37.7 percent) reached a figure considerably beyond the number of those convinced that the Chinese charges were groundless. Also with a reference to the Chinese, the *Jiji Press* took a survey in November which put the question as follows: "Communist Chinese leaders often say that militarism is reviving in Japan and is posing a

---

[28] *Mainichi Shimbun,* 12 August 1971.

threat to Asian nations. Do you think so?" The addition of the phrase "threat to Asian nations" might well have struck many of those being polled as an exaggerated conclusion which they could not accept. It was perhaps then not surprising that the results were "no," 41.8 percent; "yes," 12.3 percent; "cannot say so sweepingly," 20.2 percent; and "no opinion," 25.9 percent.

Regardless of contradictions among certain percentages in different polls, a few general observations are possible. Few accept the proposition that militarism has already revived, but at the same time few reject out of hand as ridiculous and unworthy of consideration the charges made by foreigners that a return to militarism in Japan is either going on or is a possibility for the future. Many polls show considerable division of opinion among varying responses of possibility, danger, and present fact. The uncertainty of many is apparent in the comparatively large number of "don't know" or "no answer" responses. As the commentaries have indicated, a healthy skepticism about the reality of militarism prevails, but with it exists an uneasiness about what might happen in the future.

4

Defense Policy, 1971-1972

The Fourth Defense Buildup Plan

During the latter part of 1971 and the early months of 1972, the Japanese increasingly directed their attention toward the Fourth Defense Buildup Plan, and discussions of the plan, which became heated in the Diet, government circles, and in the press, markedly influenced their attitudes toward defense. The dimensions of the plan and the defense budget for 1972-1973 were expected to be decided by 1 April 1972, the beginning of the fiscal year and the date the plan was scheduled to go into effect. Later events upset the budget timetable and delayed the plan's approval.

In 1971 Japan was eleventh in the world in defense spending and twelfth in defense manpower (see Appendix, Document 13). Should the totals planned for the Fourth Defense Buildup Plan be translated into budgets, Japan's world rank would move to seventh place, immediately after China. The amount projected for the five-year period was ¥5.8 trillion (this amount would include personnel increments) or $16.1 billion (at the 1970 rate of ¥360 to the dollar), thus producing annual budgets of approximately $3.2 billion, more than double the amount of the 1970 figure ($1.58 billion). The percentage of GNP, 0.8 percent in 1970, would advance to approximately 0.92 percent, according to projected estimates of the GNP.

During the latter half of 1971 the government's defense plans came under sharp fire. Two events occurred during July which seriously influenced attitudes toward the buildup of military strength. On July 15 President Nixon announced his planned visit to Peking which signified to the Japanese a marked change in power relationships in

Asia. This conviction was strengthened when the People's Republic of China was admitted to the United Nations in the following October. Government critics, press, and politicians spoke of a new relaxation of tensions which would make big arms expenditures less justifiable. Why should Japan vote such enormous funds for the military, ran the argument, when threats to the peace were being dissipated? A Sino-American agreement would further diminish the threat to Japan, if indeed any threat had existed in the first place.

The second event, on 30 July, was the mid-air collision of a fighter of the Air Self Defense Forces with a commercial passenger plane, resulting in 162 deaths, the largest number of casualties ever suffered up to that time in an air accident. Subsequent investigation revealed the existence of government regulations extending priority to military planes for the use of air corridors over the Japanese islands. The military plane was presumed to be at fault and the prime minister apologized to the nation. He also affirmed in the Diet that military priority in the use of air space would be withdrawn. The director-general of the Defense Agency and the commander of the Air Self Defense Forces both resigned to show responsibility for the disaster. In the ensuing public outcry, the defense establishment lost prestige and support, while the critics of an arms buildup found their position measurably strengthened.

But for the government, the most persuasive influence with respect to the proposed defense buildup was the economic depression which had already substantially reduced the growth rate and which President Nixon's economic "shock" of 15 August further aggravated. The sky-rocketing cost of defense was clear for all to see. Not only the Finance Ministry, ever-zealous guardian of the public coffers, but officials and members of the press and public began to call for retrenchment in defense expenditures on grounds of economy.

In early November, business and defense industry leaders were calling for a year's postponement in the buildup plan, and the Defense Agency immediately began to study the possibility of either curtailing the plan or postponing its scheduled start. During the month the press vigorously debated the question of what to do about the plan in the light of the rapidly changing international situation and Japan's economic slowdown.

The *Mainichi* editorialized on 2 November 1971: "we expect the government to hasten drastic restudies of the Fourth Defense Plan, including the advisability of its postponement, not for just makeshift reasons but from the standpoint of changing the image of the nation."

By "image" the *Mainichi* writer meant impressions of Japan—supposedly current in Asian and European nations, as well as the United States—as a country with tendencies toward militarism and economic aggression. Japan's image in the United States, of course, has been a mixed one.

The *Yomiuri* commented on 5 November: "the Fourth Defense Buildup Plan needs to be restudied radically owing to changes in the internal and external objective conditions, the defense concept and many other points. Implementation should be deferred on this occasion." *Sankei* on 8 November sounded a note of caution:

It is true that tension in Asia is being eased since China is taking a flexible attitude. There is no assurance, however, that China's mood for peaceful co-existence has been established firmly—the situation in Asia, though moving conspicuously in the direction of easing tension, is still very uncertain in reality.

. . . the Japanese economy has suffered a serious blow from the U.S. dollar-defense measures. This cannot be taken as an excuse, however, for reckless reduction of the (Fourth Defense Plan). On the contrary, the defense industry may be important from a new angle in a period of business recession.

According to the press, the Defense Production Committee of the Federation of Economic Organizations (*Keidanren*) agreed on 10 November 1971 that while some reductions in the defense budgets under the buildup plan might be unavoidable, no postponement of the plan's implementation could be justified. Mr. Kono Fumihiko, chairman of the committee and chairman of the board of Mitsubishi Heavy Industries, a leading Japanese defense contractor, gave a press conference on 17 November in which he described his own position in more detail. He noted that when economic growth slowed down, a retrenchment in the scale of defense spending could not be helped. He was convinced, however, that even if the international relationships should be considerably affected by a relaxation of tension in Asia, Japan would still require a powerful defensive force. He disagreed with important elements in business circles and the Liberal Democratic Party who favored postponing the plan, on the grounds that such postponement might result in the plan becoming "lost among other problems" and thus being delayed indefinitely. He appealed for a decision by Prime Minister Sato before Japan undertook aggressive efforts to normalize diplomatic relations with mainland China.

By the latter part of November, advocates of postponement seemed to have lost the battle, and the Defense Agency prepared to submit the draft plan to the cabinet for approval on the basis of its original outlines. On 10 December the finance minister, the director-general of the Defense Agency, and the chief cabinet secretary agreed that the Fourth Defense Buildup Plan would start from 1 April 1972, roughly in its original form.

As might be expected, a storm of objections greeted the go-ahead decision. The *Asahi* on 16 December, concerned over the image Japan would present to the world as a stabilizing force in Asia, called for drastic adjustments in the basic concept of the Fourth Defense Buildup Plan and demanded "again" that the government postpone the start of the plan for another year. The *Yomiuri* (13 December) also questioned the basic concept of the plan:

> At the present time, when the time of President Nixon's visit to China is close at hand, China's participation in the United Nations has been realized and the world is moving rapidly toward a tripolar structure, can it be said that there is still no need of making any alteration in the basic concept of the Fourth Defense Plan? . . . The Fourth Defense Plan should be postponed at least one year in order to watch changes in the future of the Asian situation.

Prime Minister Sato was asked about the effect of the changing situation in Asia on Japan's defense posture. He replied to a committee of the House of Representatives on 13 December: "The situation in Asia has changed greatly, through China's admission into the United Nations, etc. However, at present, it is not a situation in which we must make changes in our views regarding national defense." [1]

Criticism of the scale of the plan came from another source. The director-general of the Economic Planning Agency met the finance minister on 14 December and, according to the press, requested that in compiling the budget for FY 1972 "the scale of the Fourth Defense Buildup Plan should be studied with a view toward retrenchment, in connection with the economic growth rate." [2] In a panel discussion

---

[1] *Nihon Keizai Shimbun,* 14 December 1971.
[2] *Asahi Evening News,* 14 December 1971.

reported by the press on 11 January 1972, the director-general of the Planning Agency asserted that he did not oppose starting the plan in 1972, but he hoped that the budget for the first year could be kept fairly small, since the economic outlook would become clearer as time went on. He also expressed concern that defense be considered in the context of all aspects of the nation's economy, politics, and society. He remarked: "If the consolidation of social capital lags behind and if dissatisfaction were to become very strong within the country, what good will defense power be?" [3]

The defense budget for FY 1972 was approved by the cabinet and submitted for approval to the Diet in January of that year. The total was ¥803 billion or approximately $2.6 billion. The National Defense Council made no decision on the Fourth Defense Buildup Plan and the government expected approval only in the latter half of 1972, when economic trends could be better assessed. The Diet opposition demanded drastic reductions in the 1972 budget proposal; it contained projects drawn up by uniformed Defense Agency personnel which, in fact, were part of the five-year plan and which, if the budget were passed, would be funded before the plan itself had been approved by the National Defense Council. The Socialist, Komeito, and Democratic Socialist parties found common ground on this issue and exploited it to the maximum to try to bring down the Sato government. To exert pressure on the LDP majority, the opposition forces refused to participate in any Diet business. The result was a major parliamentary crisis which paralyzed the Diet for seventeen days.

The boycott began on 8 February when members of the principal opposition parties, Socialist, Komeito, and Democratic Socialist, walked out of the House of Representatives and party leaders announced that they would not resume their seats until (1) the government revised the defense budget and confirmed the primacy of civilian control, and (2) the prime minister apologized. Through the efforts of Speaker of the House Funada Naka, the government party and the opposition reached an agreement and the Diet returned to normal operations on 25 February. The government accepted most of the opposition's demands. It expressed regret over the fact that the FY 1972 defense budget had been related to the yet unapproved Fourth Defense Buildup Plan and agreed to take proper measures to assure effective civilian

---

[3] *Tokyo Shimbun,* 11 January 1972.

control of the defense establishment. The most substantial concessions were the agreement to eliminate budget items for the purchase of aircraft amounting to approximately $9 million (the total budget was $2.6 billion) and the decision to suspend funding of additional contracts and funding for the acquisition of aircraft, in the amount of nearly $300 million, until after the buildup plan was approved. The aircraft involved were included in the Fourth Defense Buildup Plan and hence had become a focal point of controversy.

The course and outcome of the crisis over the 1972 defense budget illustrated the power of the opposition on the defense issue over a government which, although controlling a comfortable parliamentary majority, felt it necessary to capitulate on important points in order to secure the normal functioning of the Diet. Even LDP leaders recognized that the government had committed a needless error in permitting items contained in the plan to be slipped into the 1972 budget. Government spokesmen were caught in the contradiction of trying to explain in Diet hearings that, while the budget was in no way connected with the still unapproved plan, the 1972 appropriation would in fact be equivalent to the first year of the plan. Opposition spokesmen were quick to accuse uniformed professionals in the Defense Agency of blatantly ignoring the principle of civilian control by trying to increase their own appropriations through getting the plan activated before it had been properly considered and sanctioned. Anxiety over the economic situation stemming from President Nixon's new economic policy and from the yen revaluation, combined with the general mood of international détente encouraged by the President's planned visits to Peking and Moscow, provided the opposition with greater impetus to clamor for reduced defense expenditures. Always with a view to the ending of Prime Minister Sato's term, Socialist, DSP, and Komeito leaders looked ahead to elections expected in 1972, and knew that they were sponsoring a popular cause.

With the 1972 budget passed, the pressure was off for quick approval of the Fourth Defense Buildup Plan. Its total amount was not finally settled until 9 October 1972, when the cabinet fixed the five-year program at ¥4.6 trillion ($15.4 billion at the 1972 exchange rate). Total expenditures would probably reach $17 billion because of expected rises in personnel costs.[4]

---

[4] *Japan Times,* 10 October 1972.

Those who look closely at Japan's Self Defense Forces agree that their strength is not a matter of money alone. In fact a far more serious problem is personnel. The present armed forces are said to be under-manned by 24,000 men; the vacancies in the Ground Self Defense Forces now amount to more than 13 percent. Furthermore, it is diffi-cult to train men to handle the increasingly complex modern weaponry which is being acquired. Morale among defense force personnel is going down; the caliber of young recruits is inferior and those who enter the forces find little to inspire them. Without a clear objective and without even a credible hypothetical enemy, it is hard to instill military spirit in the men who serve. In a country with a shortage of manpower, and a multitude of opportunities offered by private busi-ness and industry, mainly the second-raters are left to joint the SDF.

In early 1973 the Defense Agency submitted a draft plan called "Goal for the Consolidation of Defense Power in Peacetime," which specified that Japan's level of defense should "contribute to the stabiliza-tion of international relations and, coupled with the U.S.-Japan security treaty, by expressing the country's determination to defend its indepen-dence and peace, act as a deterrent to prevent the easy development of aggressive intentions against our country." The plan was based on the premise that "in addition to constitutional and policy restrictions" expenditures would be limited to within 1 percent of GNP. The forces envisaged under the plan would be as follows:

Ground Self Defense Forces	3 area armies, 13 divisions, 180,000 men.
Maritime Self Defense Forces	5 regional units, 4 to 5 es-cort flotillas, 250,000 to 280,000 tons.
Air Self Defense Forces	3 regional air defense forces, 8 air wings, about 800 planes.[5]

Japanese Sharing of American Defense Costs

The fact that Japan's armed forces originated at the time of the out-break of the Korean War and during the occupation made it natural

---

[5] *Nihon Keizai Shimbun* (evening edition), 1 February 1973.

that their military equipment should in the beginning be American-made and, after 1954, furnished under the military assistance program. The Japanese defense industry dates from this period when Japan became a source for the American procurement of necessary materiel and services. The industry has grown, but even in recent years has accounted for no more than 0.4 percent of Japan's total industrial production. Mitsubishi Heavy Industries, the largest supplier to the SDF, produces more than 30 percent of Japan's domestic defense equipment; yet these sales represented in 1970 only 4 percent of the company's total sales.

In July 1970 the Defense Agency issued a policy statement which declared that defense power should be based on the nation's industrial power, that the domestic development and production of military equipment should be promoted, that emphasis should be placed on utilizing the developmental and technical resources of private industry, and that the principle of competition should be encouraged. The last provision was intended to prevent a few companies from monopolizing defense industry. In August 1970 the defense production committee of the Federation of Economic Organizations (*Keidanren*) issued its own policy statement in which it endorsed the stand on domestic production and on research and development for military equipment. Also in 1970, Defense Agency Director-General Nakasone stated that a goal of the Fourth Defense Buildup Plan should be to reach 80 percent domestic production of all military equipment. The draft of the plan specified that 19 percent of the budget for principal items should be in foreign currency.

In the years during and after the phasing out of the military assistance program, the United States urged Japan to purchase more American military equipment. The stated purposes were not only to assist the American balance-of-payments deficit, but also to modernize the SDF and to enable a more fully armed Japan to assume greater defense responsibilities.

In 1971 after Secretary of Defense Laird's summer visit to Japan and President Nixon's August announcement of his economic policy, discussion of further Japanese sharing in American defense costs grew in intensity, but the Japanese press and public greeted the idea with little enthusiasm. A *Sankei* poll reported on 12 October found that 55 percent of those queried saw no need for Japan to share American military costs in Japan. Six percent found it natural for Japan to shoulder such expenses in return for protection by the United States, and 31 percent approved "within the limits of Japan's economic capacity."

The proposals to buy more American military equipment were taken much more seriously; they provoked heated discussions by defense commentators, industrialists, and politicians. The question was clearly posed: would it be in Japan's interest to concentrate almost exclusively on domestic production or should imports of military equipment be increased?

For some time, critics—even some within the Defense Agency—had exposed the many myths relating to domestic production (*kokusan*). Chauvinism had led to exaggerations of the percentages of equipment made in Japan. In many instances Japan was importing all vital parts and merely assembling them in Japan. As Kaihara Osamu, chief of the secretariat of the National Defense Council, described it, "It is like buying a model airplane and putting it together." Lack of experience, inferior research and development, and the absence of mass production meant that imported equipment was usually of better quality and cheaper in price than that domestically produced.

Needless to say, industrialists engaged in defense production argued vigorously against building up imports only to become dependent on them. They cited the goal of "autonomous defense" as natural for any independent nation and noted the dangers of being at the mercy of foreign countries in a time of emergency. One cited the case of Sweden which found outside sources of supply cut off at the beginning of World War II and as a result immediately had to set to work to build a strong and independent arms industry.

Closely allied to the question of domestic production was the encouragement of research and development for which the Fourth Defense Buildup Plan included a budget 3.58 times larger than that of the previous plan. Proponents of *kokusan* stressed not only the importance of research and development for the defense industry but also its beneficial effects on nonmilitary production. The policy of 1970 had stated, "autonomous defense starts with autonomous technology."

Yet imported equipment cost less, and this price advantage had great appeal to Japan, especially in a period of economic difficulty. For example, the cost of a Japan-built fighter training plane was said to be ¥1.4 billion ($4.5 million) whereas a plane of similar characteristics and capabilities manufactured in the United States by the Northrup Company would cost slightly more than half this price or ¥700 million ($2.5 million). The Ministry of Finance was naturally interested in reducing costs, and it favored the purchase of cheaper weapons imported from the United States. The revaluation of the yen added to this advantage. The director-general of the Defense Agency commented in December 1971 that while priority would continue to be given to research and development, the revaluation of the yen would further reduce the price of imports and an intensification of arms sales campaigns by foreign countries could be expected.

Chairman Kono of Mitsubishi Heavy Industries discussed the question of domestic production and imports in a press conference in Tokyo on 13 January 1972. Kono's position as a leader of the industrialists engaged in defense production lent authority to his views. Kono repeated the principle that domestic production should be basic government policy, but he admitted that in the interest of Japanese-American relations, Japan should assume some defense costs, or their equivalent, which had been borne by the United States. He proposed the purchase of American-made weapons as long as it did not hinder domestic production, the purchase of medium-term bonds, and an increase in economic cooperation programs. Kono suggested that what could be done to "appease" the Americans by these methods was limited, and he was obviously unenthusiastic about large increases in the imports of weapons. He then made the rather remarkable suggestion, which he termed his "personal view," that Japan, to meet the insistent American demand that she share defense costs, should offer to pay the United States an annual fee of from $200 to $300 million for the "nuclear umbrella" provided by the United States for the security of Japan!

Kono himself was not optimistic that the Japanese government would take up his suggestion (he said they lacked the courage); in any case his proposal was greeted with little public enthusiasm. He stressed that since the defense industry did not want to sacrifice domestic production for the sake of boosting imports, "We had better pay with money!" *Nihon Keizai* commented on 14 January 1972 that paying rent for a "nuclear umbrella" not only might break down the ban on the entry or possession of nuclear weapons but would also arouse strong public opposition.

The problem of how much to import and how much to produce domestically may never be satisfactorily resolved for all concerned. Pressures from industry and from those who see Japanese independence and "autonomous defense" tied with "autonomous technology" and "domestic weapons production" will compete with those—principally elements within the government, those directly concerned with finance and those concerned with Japan's relations with the United States—who are persuaded to look to imports by considerations of economy and international relations.

Certainly Japan's defense industry has great capacity for growth and, if the appropriate policy decisions were to be made, production of military equipment for export could become an attractive and profitable enterprise. Japan's high level of technology, including its applications in the steel and electronics industries, suggests a potentially encouraging future. Especially if costs can be reduced, the domestic production of equipment for the Self Defense Forces may be expected to advance moderately in the coming years. Should a decision ever be made to embark on a program of full rearmament, the defense industry would be able to rise to the occasion.

The Defense of Okinawa

In the joint communiqué of 21 November 1969 in which President Nixon and Prime Minister Sato agreed on the return to Japan of the administrative rights over Okinawa, the prime minister "made clear the intention of his government, following reversion, to assume gradually the responsibility for the immediate defense of Okinawa as part of Japan's defense efforts for her own territories" (see Appendix, Document 7). Following the signing of the reversion agreement between Japan and the United States on 17 June 1971, the Defense Agency and the senior U.S. military representative in Tokyo signed an "arrangement" for Japan's assumption of the "immediate defense" of Okinawa. The arrangement specified the forces to be deployed by Japan in assuming "the mission for the immediate defense of Okinawa, namely, ground defense, air defense, maritime defense patrol and search and rescue to be assigned by the Japanese Defense Agency (JDA)." Assumption of the mission was to take place as soon as practicable after reversion but not later than 1 July 1973. The initial deployment was to consist of approximately 3,200 personnel within six months after reversion, to be made up of elements from the Ground, Air, and Maritime Self Defense Forces. The installations where deployment was to be made were specified in the agreement.

71

According to Japanese press reports in January 1972, the JDA had decided to send 600 men to Okinawa on 15 May, the day of reversion, and to have 3,000 there within six months. By the end of the Fourth Defense Buildup Plan on 1 April 1977, the total strength of the Self Defense Forces deployed in Okinawa was to be 6,500.

Most Americans would conclude that for Japan to become responsible for the immediate defense of Okinawa would be a natural move which should be welcomed in Japan and Okinawa since it would permit the Americans to relinquish certain military installations in the islands. The Japanese government expected that a defense role in Okinawa would be normal. Most Japanese, excepting those who opposed defense in general and who saw the extension of Japanese military control in Okinawa as a step toward militarism, found the stationing of the SDF in Okinawa an inevitable consequence of reversion. Okinawan reaction was different. Many Okinawans saw members of the Self Defense Forces as the reincarnation of the cruel and arrogant imperial troops they had known under Japanese control before and during the Second World War. The image was not a happy one.

The reversion movement was fanned for many years with the slogan "Return to the Homeland!", a powerful political catalyst for opposition parties, groups, and movements. But now that reversion was a certainty, enthusiasm gave way to doubts. Robert A. Fearey, civil administrator of Okinawa, discussed the reversion agreement in a speech delivered in Naha, 13 October 1971:

> It is a good agreement, carefully negotiated, which won substantial approval in the U.S. and Japan. But in Okinawa, though the agreement brought the long-sought goal of reversion much closer, and though every effort was made in the negotiations to take account of Okinawan desires, enthusiasm is, as you will have observed, restrained. Feelings are ambivalent, with many Okinawans showing uneasiness and tension as they look in the future.

Much of the uneasiness in Okinawa is due to the continued maintenance there of American military bases and personnel. But the people of the Ryukyus also harbor deep anxiety about policies to be pursued by their new Japanese masters and about the deployment of the Self Defense Forces. Fearey asks, but does not answer, the question, "What problems will the introduction of the Japan SDF present?"

Political attitudes in Okinawa are colored by the fact that the chief executive, Yara Chobyo, was elected by the "reformist" elements and has therefore been strongly critical of the reversion agreement, while a majority in the legislature is controlled by the Okinawan Liberal Democratic Party (OLDP), related to the governing LDP in Japan, which has promoted and supported the agreement. While even the supporters of the agreement found much to criticize in it, they insisted that revision should be sought *after* the first goal, reversion, had been accomplished. "Reformist" opponents of the agreement, whose principal aim was to abolish the American bases, were demanding its revision *before* signature and ratification.

As the time for reversion approached, Japan began to replace the United States as a target of opposition protest, and one of the vivid symbols of the impending return of Japanese rule was the prospect of Japanese Self Defense Forces in the islands. Older Okinawans recalled indignities and cruelties suffered at the hands of the old Imperial Army. Harking back to prewar memories, they envisaged an old-time Japanese army returning under the camouflage of a "self-defense force" label. Signs appeared on the streets of Naha: "Stop the Stationing of Self Defense Forces!" A leading Japanese magazine sent researchers to gather testimonials from one hundred Okinawans who had suffered at the hands of the Japanese military and published a special section entitled, "What Have Japanese Soldiers Done to Okinawa?" [6] From those interviewed the magazine's representatives repeatedly heard the view that the "supposedly friendly Japanese military forces were worse than the American enemies." The one hundred personal, blood-curdling accounts of atrocities perpetrated by Japanese soldiers in Okinawa were hardly a comforting preparation for the SDF entry in 1972.

But there is more to the Okinawans' anxiety over their Japanese future than memories of the old Japanese army. Although in American terms the concept of the Ryukyus as the "keystone" of the Pacific was logical and credible, the American administrators of Okinawa were never able successfully to inculcate in the Okinawan people a sense of Okinawa's strategic contribution to Pacific security. Many Okinawans still believed that the Japanese, simply by fortifying Okinawa before the war with the United States, had drawn the Americans to fight the decisive battle of the war against Japan on Okinawan soil and in the

---

[6] *Ushio,* vol. 146 (November 1971), pp. 92-227.

process to kill some 115,000 Okinawan civilians. With American bases still maintained and a new Japanese military force now appearing, many inhabitants believe that their land could again become part of a re-militarized Japan—again a magnet to embroil them in the tragedy of war. Thus, talk about a revival of Japanese militarism seems less incredible to Okinawans than to their compatriots in the homeland.

Those who think further into the future are speculating now about the effect of Japan's assumption of Okinawa's immediate defense on the security of wider areas of the western Pacific. The southernmost Ryukyu Islands are within sight of Taiwan. Japan's Maritime Self Defense Force will have the role of patrolling the waters around the Ryukyu Islands. Already, prominent Japanese have discussed the potential threats to the sea lanes so necessary to Japan's vital trade with Southeast Asia and, more important, to the essential oil route through the Malacca Strait to the Persian Gulf. Responsible Japanese officials, such as Nakasone Yasuhiro, formerly and later minister of trade and industry, and Ohira Masayoshi, the present foreign minister, have warned that a sure defense of Japan's far-flung sea routes is impractical. Therefore, how to cope with threats arising near the defense perimeters of the Self Defense Forces could become a problem for Japan in the future.

One possible source of conflict is the Senkaku Islands, recognized as part of the Ryukyus by the United States and Japan but claimed as Chinese territory by the governments of both the People's Republic of China and the Republic of China on Taiwan. Should the predictions of rich, offshore oil resources prove correct, China's challenge to Japanese sovereignty over the Senkakus could seriously disturb future relations between Peking and Tokyo.

The immediate problem for Japan, however, has been the opposition of the Okinawans to the deployment of the SDF which began after 15 May 1972. The nature of the reaction was predicted by a public opinion poll taken by the *Asahi Shimbun* in cooperation with the *Okinawa Times* on 27–28 August 1971. Whereas in Japan 54 percent of the respondents favored the deployment of Japanese forces in Okinawa against 25 percent who opposed it, in Okinawa the figures were almost reversed, with 56 percent *opposed* to the stationing of Japanese forces and only 22 percent in favor. The SDF were well aware of the problems they had to face. Members of the Okinawan "Council for Reversion to the Fatherland" announced that they would use force to stop the "landing" of the first elements of the SDF. To smooth the way, the Japanese gvernment established a budget of about $4,000 for public relations. Marching bands of the respective ground, sea, and air forces were to be sent to the islands, and festivals and exhibitions were to be sponsored in an effort to improve the "image" of the arriving troops.

Prime Minister Sato, when questioned in the upper house of the Diet by a Socialist member who accused the government of failing to understand the "heart of Okinawa" in deploying Japanese armed forces there, replied: "It is understandable that from their abnormal experience during and after the war, the Okinawan prefectural people have a special feeling toward the SDF. However, the deployment of SDF is indispensable for securing the safety of the Okinawan prefectural people and extending disaster relief." [7]

Actually the entry of the first SDF contingents was accomplished without violent resistance from the Okinawans. Still, resentment at yet another military "presence" has not died and in late 1972 Naha streets were still decorated with signs: "Japanese Self Defense Forces Go Home!"

Changing Attitudes toward Japan's Security Policy

The Japanese recognized that the announcement of President Nixon's planned visit to Peking and the admission of the People's Republic of China to the United Nations caused immediate changes in power relationships in Asia. The "rush to China" was on—leading industrialists, businessmen, journalists, and political party delegations flocked to Peking, all meeting with Premier Chou En-lai, issuing statements thereafter, and seeking maximum time on television and space in the press on their return home. The Chinese made it clear that Prime Minister Sato—long-standing "stooge of the imperialists"—would not be welcome and, ironically, because of their long-standing ideological quarrel, neither would any representative of the Japanese Communist Party. For all other prominent Japanese, the welcome mat was out. In 1971 the "Sino-Japanese Memorandum Trade Agreement," which in the past had consumed weeks of difficult negotiations, was hammered out in Peking in a few days. Polls showed that now more Japanese were interested in cultivating China than the United States, which had won the accolade in previous years.[8] Japan was indeed in a "China mood."

---

[7] *Mainichi Shimbun* (evening edition), 15 December 1971.

[8] The *Asahi Shimbun* published its own poll on 3 January 1972 in which China received 33 percent and the U.S. 28 percent of the vote.

In this atmosphere it was natural that some Japanese should question whether the Japan-U.S. security treaty should continue in its present form, if at all. The Sato government, however, still stood behind the treaty. Having restated with President Nixon in 1969 the intention "firmly to maintain the treaty" and having survived the "crisis of 1970" when the treaty became subject to notice of termination, the prime minister continued to defend it against his opponents whose attacks became louder after the "Nixon China shock" and the entry of China into the United Nations. Yet the change in atmosphere between 1969 and 1972 led President Nixon and Prime Minister Sato to mention only in a subordinate sentence of their joint statement signed at San Clemente in January 1972 that they "highly valued" the security treaty (see Appendix, Document 11). This contrasted with their 1969 declared intent "firmly to maintain it." The pertinent passage in the 1972 statements came in the fourth paragraph:

> The Prime Minister and the President, recalling the more than 100 years of association between the two countries, emphasized the importance of U.S.-Japanese relations being founded on mutual trust and independence. In this connection, they highly valued the important role played by the Treaty of Mutual Cooperation and Security between Japan and the United States.

The elements of the 1969 Sato-Nixon communiqué which have recently drawn the sharpest attack from the opposition parties in Japan are the assertions by the prime minister that the "security of the Republic of Korea was essential to Japan's own security" and that "the maintenance of peace and security in the Taiwan area was also a most important factor for the security of Japan." Chou En-lai repeatedly singled out the latter, the so-called "Taiwan clause," as proof of a Japanese commitment to support America's defense of Taiwan. In fact, Prime Minister Sato went beyond the wording of the communiqué in a speech to the National Press Club in Washington on 21 November 1969. Discussing the security treaty requirement for prior consultation in the event of a threat which caused the United States to ask to use Japanese bases and facilities, the prime minister stated that in the case of Korea the Japanese government would decide its position "positively and promptly." An attack on Taiwan which caused American treaty commitments to be invoked would ipso facto "be a threat to the peace and security of the Far East including Japan."

In the face of fire from the Socialists and Communists in the Diet, Sato insisted that Japan had never given up the sovereign right to say either yes or no should the United States ask to use Japanese facilities under the treaty. His foes flung the Press Club speech back at him, quoting his use of "positively," a much stronger word than the original Japanese *maemuki* and unmistakably meaning a promise to say yes. Finally, in November 1971 Sato bowed to his critics and announced to the House of Representatives Special Committee on the Okinawa Reversion Agreement that he was retracting the word "positively" and would accordingly amend his Press Club speech. Since this statement had referred only to Korea, he was pressed relentlessly on Taiwan and replied somewhat vaguely: "A fire next door cannot be left unheeded. It is natural to prepare for the preventing of the fire, and although I hope that problems will not arise, we cannot remain indifferent." [9]

The Japanese journalists in San Clemente asked Sato why no mention was made of the security of Korea and Taiwan in the joint statement. The prime minister answered:

> There are no Taiwan or ROK clauses. However, the impression is too strong if this is taken as a change in policy. The security treaty structure still continues to exist, and if some situation were to arise in Taiwan or the ROK, American soldiers would probably be sent there, although Japan itself is not in a position to go itself. In such a case, this will naturally become a matter for prior consultations. The new point, however, is that it is moving in the direction where such a situation will not arise, and both Taiwan and the ROK are contained within the scope of the security treaty structure. [10]

During the same press conference a journalist asked whether the prime minister believed that his emphasis on continuing the security treaty structure would obstruct the restoration of diplomatic relations between Japan and China. Sato replied that he did not think so, and went on, "The security treaty exists as a firm reality. It has not been strengthened, but we will continue it in the future." [11]

It was clear from statements made after the San Clemente meetings by both Prime Minister Sato and Foreign Minister Fukuda that they

---

[9] Sato, quoted in *Mainichi Shimbun* (evening edition), 22 November 1971.
[10] *Asahi Shimbun* (evening edition), 8 January 1972.
[11] Ibid.

saw considerable change in the international situation since that of November 1969 when the security interests of Japan in Korea and Taiwan had been specified. In their opinion China's new position and the subsequent easing of tensions expected in Asia drastically reduced the likelihood of Japan's becoming involved in an American military action in Asia. Still, both ministers consistently affirmed the necessity to maintain the security treaty with the United States. The foreign minister described the change primarily one of "mood." He believed that the "degree" of danger for Japan had diminished but that the Republics of Korea and of China on Taiwan were still important to Japan.[12]

If the government remained staunch in its defense of the treaty, some prominent members of the governing Liberal Democratic Party were wavering. It must not be forgotten that 1972 was a political year for Japan. Sato was ending his fourth term and setting off a jostle for the succession; the positions taken by would-be prime ministers, therefore, were not without political motive. Not surprisingly, prospective candidates sought to point up their policy differences with Sato and to champion issues which they believed would evoke favorable public response. Although the security treaty in 1960 had produced the most massive riots and demonstrations in Japan's postwar history, the issue of its extension in 1970 was less explosive than had been expected and since that time it has produced few ripples on the public consciousness. Polls in recent years suggest that relatively few Japanese wish to abrogate the treaty but few also want to maintain it permanently. There appeared to be substantial popular support for the positions taken by the two middle-of-the-road political parties, the Democratic Socialists which advocate "revision through removal of U.S. bases but with a U.S. commitment to return in an emergency," and the Komeito which until recently favored "dissolution by gradual stages." [13]

Several prominent LDP politicians have publicly discussed revision of the treaty. Nakasone Yasuhiro created a stir in 1969 by speaking

---

[12] *Yomiuri Shimbun,* 9 January 1972.

[13] The Komeito in early 1973 changed its position on the treaty to favor its "immediate dissolution." This shift was no doubt a result of its own losses and the Communist party gains in the December 1972 elections. (*Asahi Shimbun,* 29 January 1973.) A poll taken on 6 and 7 April 1973 revealed only 7 percent of the respondents in favor of "immediate abolition" of the treaty; on the other hand, 71 percent supported the treaty either "as it is now" (17 percent), "with changed content" (29 percent) or "with progress in the direction of eventual abolition (25 percent). (*Asahi Shimbun,* 1 May 1973.)

publicly of replacing the security treaty with a friendship treaty, this to be accomplished in 1975. Miki Takeo, former foreign minister and deputy prime minister under Tanaka, more recently asserted the need for Japan to seek revision of the treaty with the United States. Ohira Masayoshi, foreign minister in the Tanaka cabinet, talked about Japan's "independence" from the United States when he was a candidate for the premiership and even suggested that the treaty might become an issue for the future. After taking office he did not repeat the suggestion.

One argument for the treaty, usually made by foreigners but also persuasive to many Japanese, is that should the treaty disappear—and with it the American "nuclear umbrella"—Japan would be tempted, if not forced, to produce nuclear weapons to guarantee her own security. Former Ambassador Edwin O. Reischauer has long warned that abrogation of the treaty would almost certainly drive Japan to become a nuclear power. Then Deputy Secretary of Defense David Packard reportedly told the chairman of the Japanese Democratic Socialist Party, visiting Washington in December 1971, that if the Japanese desired the withdrawal of American forces and bases from their country, the United States would restudy the security treaty system now in force. In the event of withdrawal of American forces or bases, however, Packard is said to have advised the Japanese to assume complete responsibility for their own defense, including the capability to counter China's nuclear weapons.[14]

Many responsible Japanese, deeply concerned over the risks of remilitarization, feel that Japan would run a serious risk of "going nuclear" if the protection provided by the treaty were to be removed. At the same time, some commentators stress that while most Japanese look upon the treaty solely as a deterrent against Communist aggression, Americans interpret it more as a deterrent against Japan's rearming with nuclear weapons. Such an interpretation appeared to be confirmed by an unnamed American embassy spokesman who in January 1972 was reported to have said that "one of the effects of the United States-Japan security treaty is to stem Japan's enthusiasm for nuclear development."[15] Japanese journalists were inspired to speculate on just how Americans did evaluate the treaty and drew conclusions of their own. The Sankei newspaper surmised that the United States might use the treaty as a brake to curb excessive expansion of Japan's national power

[14] *Sankei Shimbun,* 7 January 1972.
[15] *Mainichi Shimbun,* 16 January 1972.

which could pose a threat to both the United States and China. *Sankei* concluded that this might force Japan "to shoulder a 'disadvantageous role' in the policy toward China." The editorial added: "What we fear most is the possibility of distrust in the United States giving rise to narrow-minded nationalism in Japan and its leading quickly to the short-range reaction of favoring nuclear armament." [16] The *Mainichi* saw in the American belief that the treaty would prevent Japanese nuclear armament a derogation of Japanese sovereignty, an effort to "keep watch on Japan . . . a haughty statement . . . extremely unpleasant for the Japanese people." The paper asserted that Japan must determine independently her own nuclear policy.[17]

It would seem that Prime Minister Sato himself was not immune to the argument that the security treaty is good insurance against a Japanese nuclear capability. In answer to a Socialist interpellation in a Diet committee, Sato reportedly disclosed that he had asked President Nixon at San Clemente to explain to the Chinese when he went to Peking that "under the existing security treaty with the United States" Japan will never possess nuclear weapons. [18] Prime Minister Tanaka, replying to a Diet interpellation on 30 January 1973, startled his auditors by stating, "If there is no security treaty, defense power will become greater." As a result of persistent heckling by members of the opposition, he later amended his statement to read: "regardless of whether the security treaty exists or not, our country's self-defense power must be the minimum necessary amount for self defense." [19]

Changing power relationships in Asia will seriously affect Japan's security policy and Japanese attitudes toward defense. The Japanese public awaited President Nixon's visit to Peking with mixed emotions; hope for the widely predicted relaxation of tensions in East Asia was mingled with anxiety that a too-close Chinese-American relationship might impair the partnership which the Japanese thought they enjoyed with the Americans. The Chinese, on their part, would interpret a loosening of Japanese-American ties as an advantage for themselves. Meanwhile, the Soviet Union, clearly worried about Chinese success in breaking into the world, has unsurprisingly begun to actively cultivate Japan.

---

[16] *Sankei Shimbun,* 19 January 1972.
[17] *Mainichi Shimbun,* 15 January 1972.
[18] *Jiji Press* (Tokyo), 4 February 1972.
[19] *Asahi Evening News,* 30 January 1973.

For some months in 1972 Moscow propaganda directed against the revival of Japanese militarism had markedly softened. Much more was said about the benefits of cooperation in trade and economic development. The Japanese were pleasantly surprised when, without much prior notice, the visit to Tokyo of Foreign Minister Gromyko was announced. They were also pleased when after four days of discussions (24–27 January 1972) Gromyko did not insist on the usual public denial that a territorial issue with Japan existed. The joint communiqué ignored the question of territory. Furthermore, the parties agreed that discussions looking toward the signature of a peace treaty would begin within the year. The prospect was particularly welcome for the Japanese who, after Okinawa, regarded the return of the northern islands as their last remaining inheritance from the war.

During January 1972, simultaneously with steps to improve relations with the Soviet Union and the People's Republic of China, the Japanese moved to increase their trade relations with North Korea. A parliamentary delegation headed by a member of the ruling LDP signed a trade agreement in Pyongyang on 23 January. Trade with the Democratic People's Republic of Korea would henceforth be conducted on the same basis as that with China; according to speculation, it might expand almost ten times, from $57 million in 1970 to over $500 million by 1976. As was to be expected, the Republic of Korea reacted strongly to the new agreement; the Foreign Ministry in Seoul issued a statement on 24 January warning that if the agreement were implemented it would help North Korea build up its military capability and thus seriously affect the security of the ROK.[20] Favorable reaction to the North Korean agreement could be expected in Japan, however, given the general mood of détente within the country.

Since threats to Japan's security are presumed to come largely from China, the Soviet Union, or Korea, most Japanese understandably interpret optimistically a situation in which the United States is withdrawing from Asia, developing friendly relations with China, negotiating with the Soviet Union to maintain a nuclear balance, and bringing war in Southeast Asia to an end, and in which Japan's opportunities to improve relations with China, the U.S.S.R., and North Korea—not to speak of North Vietnam—look better than ever. This atmosphere naturally has a direct effect on attitudes toward national defense.

[20] *Asahi Shimbun,* 25 January 1972.

5
Nuclear Armament

The "Nuclear Allergy"

The origin of the "nuclear allergy" in Hiroshima and Nagasaki, its development and stimulation in the *Gensuikyo* years (1954–1960), and its gradual diminution thereafter have been mentioned earlier. Japan's more realistic attitude toward the use of nuclear energy, together with a resurgence of the national pride, the buildup of defense capacity, and unprecedented economic success have, as we have noted, aroused apprehensions about the revival of militarism, especially among observers outside Japan.

Speculation that Japan might arm with nuclear weapons has continued in spite of repeated denials by Prime Minister Sato and his steadfast reiteration of Japan's three nonnuclear principles since December 1967. Such speculation was naturally stimulated by the fact that technologically Japan could "go nuclear" very quickly should the political decision to do so be made. The Japanese now possess a highly developed atomic industry based on the application of nuclear energy for peaceful purposes. This industry grew during the *Gensuikyo* years with relatively little opposition from *Gensuikyo* and its supporters except in its earliest beginnings in 1957. In the 1960s the Japanese also made considerable progress in experimental rocketry, finally orbiting an earth satellite in February 1970, two months before the Chinese performed a similar feat. Experts conclude that given this kind of technical experience, Japan could develop a workable guided missile with a nuclear warhead within a year or two of a decision to go ahead.

The idea of nuclear weapons for Japan is relatively recent. No responsible Japanese publicly discussed such a possibility before the Chinese Communists began their nuclear testing program, except to refer to it as unthinkable. The Japanese have a long record of direct, and sometimes violent, protest against alleged United States attempts to introduce nuclear weapons into the country and against their presence in U.S.-administered Okinawa. This kind of protest came into prominence as early as 1955 when the United States, in what must have been one of the worst-timed press releases of the century, announced that the army would deploy the Honest John rocket to Japan on the day before a crucial vote to establish the Constitutional Research Council and the National Defense Council came before the House of Councillors. As a result of the announcement, the Diet adjourned in an uproar, effectively dashing all hope for Hatoyama's constitutional reform and delaying the formation of both the NDC and the Constitutional Research Council until the following year. Since that day leftist and pacifist protests against U.S. nuclear weapons, the entry of American ships which might carry them, and the visits of nuclear-powered submarines became time-honored traditions.

Hatoyama's pronouncement on the Honest John opened an era of government-opposition dialogue on nuclear weapons. Hatoyama told the Diet then that he might approve entry of atomic weapons for the defense of Japan under exceptional circumstances, but that he did not think the circumstances in 1955 justified their entry. In 1957 Prime Minister Kishi answered Diet interpellations by stating that, in his opinion, the Constitution did not prohibit nuclear weapons for defense, but from the humanitarian standpoint and because of popular sentiment, Japan's policy would be to eschew nuclear arms. In April 1958 the Kishi government, in order to allay popular fears about the introduction of the nonnuclear Sidewinder missile, clarified the difference between nuclear and nonnuclear weapons as follows: Weapons capable of being fitted with nuclear warheads are nuclear weapons only when so equipped, like the Honest John; other weapons which have no conventional adaptations, like the IRBM, are nuclear weapons. In 1970 the Defense Agency's white paper reiterated the opinion that small, tactical nuclear weapons would not be unconstitutional (see Appendix, Document 9).

With the revision of the Japan-U.S. security treaty, the Japanese inserted the "important changes in equipment" clause into the prior consultation agreement accompanying the revised treaty (see Appendix, Document 5), in effect making the introduction of nuclear weapons into Japan subject to the approval of the Japanese government. In 1962 Prime Minister Ikeda Hayato told the Diet that when Okinawa reverted to Japan (as promised by President Kennedy), it would be his government's policy to insist that there be no nuclear weapons on the islands. The problem of nuclear weapons on Okinawa, however, still remained unsettled in the minds of the Japanese. Assuming that the U.S. forces on Okinawa had nuclear weapons and fearing that when Japan received Okinawa in 1972 these weapons would still be on the islands through a rumored "secret deal" between the government and the U.S., many Japanese saw a danger, once the precedent was set, that the Americans would proceed to "Okinawa-ize" Japan. Talk of this kind diminished somewhat and fears receded with the announcement in September 1970 that the B-52s would leave Okinawa. However, anxiety did not end until October 1971 when Secretary of State Rogers and Deputy Secretary of Defense Packard gave public assurance that there would be no nuclear weapons stored on Okinawa after reversion.

The JSP sought formal Diet resolutions against nuclear weapons on many occasions over the years, the first time in April 1958, but the primary target of these early unsuccessful proposals was really the United States. The possibility that Japan might acquire nuclear weapons became realistic only after Chinese nuclear testing had begun in 1964. In December 1967 Prime Minister Sato enlarged Kishi's two principles, which were not to arm with nuclear weapons or allow these to be brought into Japan, to include "manufacture" on the prohibited list. In 1968 Sato combined his three nonnuclear principles into one in his "four pillar" nuclear policy; the others were: to work for nuclear disarmament preparatory to the complete prohibition of nuclear arms, to depend upon the United States for the nuclear deterrent, and to make the peaceful use of nuclear energy a priority national policy. In an LDP press release which appeared on 8 March 1968 the party expressed its desire that nuclear power should be used only for peaceful uses with the hope that nuclear weapons would eventually be banished from the earth together with all arms.

The opposition parties continued to press Sato and the LDP on the nuclear weapons question, but on 24 November 1971 the LDP turned the tables by joining with the Komeito and DSP to pass a Komeito nonnuclear resolution in the lower house of the Diet without the support of either the JSP or JCP. The *Resolution against Nuclear Weapons and for the Reduction of U.S. Military Bases on Okinawa* stated (in part) as follows: "The Government should observe the three nonnuclear principles . . . and should verify by proper means at the time of the reversion of Okinawa that nuclear weapons are not present on Okinawa and make clear that it will not permit the reintroduction of these weapons after reversion." [1]

Why Japan Might "Go Nuclear"

Since the Constitution, as interpreted by the government and ruling party, does not prohibit defensive nuclear weapons, a Japanese government, by reversing determined government policy and amending laws controlling the uses of atomic energy, could develop nuclear weapons "for defense" within a relatively short period of time. There are several considerations which might persuade Japan to follow this course of action. First, there is the matter of prestige. The nuclear powers clearly dominate the world political scene. One might argue that to enter this exclusive club, Japan must possess nuclear weapons; to wield political power commensurate with great economic power, the nation must "go nuclear." The Japanese could point to the recent entry of the People's Republic of China into a permanent seat on the U.N. Security Council as an example. In seating the P.R.C. the U.N. ejected the Security Council's only nonnuclear permanent member, the Republic of China. Now permanent membership appears reserved for the world's nuclear powers. The choice to seat nuclear China was made by nonnuclear nations. Should another power such as India or Israel build a nuclear arsenal, the prestige argument would become more persuasive even though neither country would pose a military threat to Japan.

A second reason would be a significant loss of credibility in the American nuclear deterrent for Japan. No United States government, this argument goes, could risk a Chicago to protect a Tokyo in the threat of a nuclear exchange. This "Gallois" idea has been used in Japan by the Socialists as a reason to abrogate the Japan-U.S. security treaty and by the advocates of domestic nuclear armament alike. According to Japan's small minority of nuclear hawks, Japan, like France, must

---

[1] *Asahi Shimbun*, 23 November 1971.

become independent of the United States for defense and must possess her own nuclear deterrent force as the best way to insure the protection of the nation from any nuclear threat. Ironically, were the outspokenly antinuclear, antiwar Socialists to succeed in their long-cherished goal of destroying the Japan-U.S. security arrangement, they might, at the same time, enhance the reasonableness of this argument for Japan to produce her own nuclear deterrent. However, a nuclear deterrent today presumes a second-strike capability; this, in turn, means the intermediate-range ballistic missile or the intercontinental ballistic missile. By every current standard the Japanese consider these to be offensive weapons prohibited by the Constitution.

A third reason for Japan to develop nuclear armament would be an increased perception of a nuclear threat, possibly from China or the Soviet Union, or, under remotely conceivable circumstances, the United States. Any argument based on a strong threat-perception presumes a loss of confidence in the American nuclear deterrent and increased tension between Japan and one or more of her possible nuclear adversaries. But the fact is that Japanese perceptions of such a threat remain quite low. For example, in a poll reported in *Yoron Chosa,* July 1970, which asked about the danger of Japan's being attacked by "a foreign country," 46.9 percent of the respondents saw slight danger, as against 11.8 percent who saw considerable danger and 18.8 percent almost no danger. An earlier government poll in September 1969 asked whether people thought war might be waged against Japan, or Japan might be involved in war (which would include being dragged into war by the Japan-U.S. security treaty). In this instance, 25 percent had reported "danger" and 27 percent "some danger." When a newspaper poll (*Yomiuri,* 31 May 1970) asked, with a direct reference to China's artificial satellite "capable of delivering nuclear weapons," whether or not citizens thought China a threat to Japan, only 18.6 percent felt the threat strongly, while 39.8 percent felt the threat "to some extent"; but the tenor of other answers in this same poll tended to give the impression that the respondents viewed the threat as stemming not entirely from Chinese attitudes, but in part from the stand of the Japanese government. Another question in this poll asked if there was danger that Japan would have a war with another country in the near future. In answer, only 7.6 percent recognized "very great danger," while 37.9 percent saw some danger, 28.7 percent little danger, and 11.3 percent no danger.

A fourth reason to possess nuclear weapons might be their appeal as instruments of international politics, to increase Japan's bargaining power with other nations.

The feeling is still strong among the Japanese that the nuclear powers aim their weapons at each other rather than at Japan, but early Chinese nuclear tests did call public attention to the nature of the nuclear threat and caused the Japanese to consider seriously for the first time the possibility that another nation's nuclear weapons might again be turned in their direction. Heightened tension between China and Japan, especially if accompanied in Japan by a loss of credibility in the U.S. intention to extend nuclear protection, would probably push Japan closer to nuclear armament. Such credibility may be further diminished when China acquires an ICBM capable of striking the United States, a likelihood in the 1970s. On the other hand, the Japanese view the current fluid world diplomatic situation as holding considerable promise of lessening tension between China and the United States as the United States gradually withdraws its power from the periphery of China. Meanwhile, the Soviet Union and the United States continue talks to reduce the level of strategic arms. All in all, the short-term prospect is that apparently reduced tensions in the East Asian area will further weaken the appeal of nuclear weapons for Japan.

Why Japan Will Not "Go Nuclear"

Professor Albert Wohlstetter of the University of Chicago has stated, "Proponents of the general spread of independent nuclear forces have greatly understated all the difficulties—the money costs, the length of time, and the political-military hazards—of independently developing and deploying a nuclear force capable of surviving an attack by a massive nuclear power, such a Russia." [2] Certainly, in the case of Japan, these difficulties exist in abundance.

The most convincing argument against nuclear weapons for Japan is her vulnerability to outside attack and the resulting difficulty in achieving a second-strike capability. A few well-placed bombs could inflict catastrophic damage on Japan's concentrated cities and industrial areas, not to speak of the casualties among the highly urbanized population. Any possible Japanese retaliation against an attack by either

[2] Albert Wohlstetter, "Japan's Security: Balancing after the Shocks," *Foreign Policy,* Winter 1972-73, p. 178.

China or Russia would be inconsequential in comparison. Even if Japan were to have built a formidable submarine fleet armed with Polaris-type or Poseidon missiles, her resulting capability to strike targets on the Asian continent would scarcely avoid or compensate for the destruction of Japanese cities. Japanese leaders, including those in the military, have for some time been pointing out Japan's vulnerability and lack of a second-strike capability. In 1972 the director-general of the Defense Bureau within the Defense Agency testified before a committee of the House of Councillors that from a purely military analysis his office had concluded that there is no justification for the use of nuclear weapons.[3]

Any Japanese leadership contemplating a transition to the status of nuclear power would calculate the expense, the domestic repercussions, and the effect on the country's international relations, particularly the reactions of neighbors in East Asia and of the United States.

Although, as we have stated, Japan is technologically capable of quickly producing atomic weapons, to do so would require a major monetary commitment and the assurance of adequate supplies of uranium over an extended period of time. So far the Japanese have been able to secure supplies of uranium from the United States and have engaged in research on the enrichment process, looking toward nuclear energy as a source of electric power. A massive effort would be required to carry out successfully a nuclear weapons program. Channeling resources in the direction of defense would mean a shift in priorities away from those goals which have been proclaimed by the government and enthusiastically supported by the public: social security, welfare, housing, education, and improvement of the environment.

A Japanese government embarking on a nuclear weapons program would obviously be sensitive to the domestic political reactions to such a venture. Unless we are to assume a dramatic shift in political power toward a conservative, hawkish majority, or toward a leadership which could ignore public opinion, domestic political opposition would be a heavy brake on the adoption of a policy of nuclear armament. But because the elections of December 1972 registered startling gains by both Communists and Socialists, the prospect of continuing resistance to a magnified arms program seems certain. Prime Minister Tanaka, who assured the Diet in November 1972 that he would oppose Japan's acquisition of nuclear weapons, faced bitter opposition to the defense

---

[3] *Yomiuri Shimbun,* 19 May 1972.

budget which fit into the Fourth Defense Buildup Plan. The traditional, strong reluctance to force bills through the Diet at the expense of a disruption of parliamentary proceedings would deter any prime minister from sponsoring a proposal so drastic as to call for the possession of nuclear arms. Still reeling from the shock of the Communist party gains in December and from the increasingly aggressive stance of the Diet opposition, the Liberal Democratic Party for a long time to come will be in no mood to risk political disaster by even suggesting that Japan should take the nuclear road.

A nuclear-armed Japan would seriously disturb the country's neighbors in Asia. "Going nuclear" would inevitably suggest a new military force in Asia and—regardless of whether the conclusion were justified—would create the severest anxieties that Japan had become a serious threat to the security and stability of these nations. In spite of Chou En-lai's reportedly mellowing attitude toward Japanese defense policies, Chinese leaders would react violently to a military resurgence in Japan to include nuclear weapons. Already the suspicions and mistrust of Japan are evident in Southeast Asia; for Japan to go nuclear would confirm the worst suspicions of the Southeast Asians, further alienate the Japanese from them, and drive them to seek economic and political support elsewhere. Japan's industrial leaders, except perhaps for a few actively engaged in defense industry, have taken public stands against a nuclear program. They have considered the possibly damaging effect of such an effort on Japan's economic relations. As Iwasa Yoshizane, vice-president of the powerful *Keidanren* (Federation of Industrial Organizations), wrote in 1970: "nuclear armament merely to placate shallow nationalism would intensify the discord with Communist China to an ominous degree and, at the same time, nullify what good will has been built up in Southeast Asia." [4] Wakaizumi Kei, a well-known Japanese specialist in defense matters, agrees that the effect on other nations would be grave:

> Various nations are still feeling the traumatic effects of World War II and are still unable to shake off the nightmare of a "militaristic Japan." They are strongly opposed to Japan's nuclear armament. . . . If nuclear armament is a means to assure a nation's security against international tension, then

---

[4] Iwasa Yoshizane, "Japan-U.S. Economic Cooperation," *Pacific Community,* April 1970, p. 389.

what is the "tension" that requires nuclear armament that will create a new tension? [5]

Of key importance will be Japan's relationship with the United States. As we have stated, an abandonment of Japan by the United States, including abrogation of the security treaty and total military withdrawal from East Asia, would profoundly affect Japan's security decisions and might well lead Japan to opt for nuclear armament and full remilitarization. Such a development, however, hardly seems likely in the foreseeable future. In spite of her Vietnam experience, the United States shows every sign of maintaining substantial interests in East Asia. While American military bases and forces will be further reduced in Japan—and Okinawa—both the Japanese and United States governments will wish to keep an American presence in Japan and to continue their cooperative defense relationship. Repeated statements by responsible American and Japanese leaders invariably stress this determination. Thus the security treaty will probably continue in effect and a situation which might impel Japan to undertake nuclear armament on her own may not develop. At the same time, it is clearly in the American interest for Japan not to rearm in a nuclear sense. Proliferation of nuclear weapons can bring no benefit to the United States, and a Japanese decision to acquire such weapons would only introduce new tensions in the Japanese-American relationship. To any suggestion that Japan might develop the bomb in cooperation with the United States, one can only say that such a hypothesis presupposes a threat of the gravest dimensions to both American and Japanese interests, as well as a complete change in the view of Asia as seen by both Washington and Tokyo.

Some observers postulate the acquisition of nuclear weapons by Japan as a normal sequence without accompanying remilitarization and without inspiring fears and apprehensions either in the Japanese body politic or abroad. Such a development might be expected were it not for Japan's aggressive past, the strength of the political opposition, and the general abhorrence, shared by most Japanese, of a return of militaristic power or control. It is difficult to imagine such a momentous decision being taken in a calm atmosphere. Some new perception of threat, some traumatic shock, would be necessary to push the Japanese leadership into such a decision. As we have concluded, such a shock

---

[5] Wakaizumi Kei, "Japan's Role," *Foreign Affairs*, January 1973, pp. 313-314.

is conceivable, and we must take account of this contingency. But without it, "going nuclear" appears unlikely in the foreseeable future.

Japan has, however, kept her options open. By interpretation rather than revision, the strictures of the Constitution's Article 9 do not obstruct the maintaining of a defense establishment; they have, however, prevented the stationing of Japanese military forces outside the country. Also by interpretation, the possession of nuclear weapons "for defense only" is not unconstitutional. The life-and-death necessity to provide adequate sources of energy for the future make the access to, and development of, nuclear technology imperative for Japan. Presumably, then, no lack of technology would hinder a transition from the peaceful to the military use of nuclear energy. At the time of the signing of the nuclear nonproliferation treaty on 3 February 1970, the Japanese government expressed a hope for nuclear disarmament agreements between the nuclear powers, for effective measures to guarantee the security of nonnuclear nations, and for equal treatment in a safeguards agreement to be concluded with the International Atomic Energy Agency. The Japanese have been concerned that no obstacle be placed on their use of atomic energy for peaceful purposes and that they not be discriminated against in relation to other nonnuclear nations.

A Japanese decision to go nuclear would be a political decision. It would be based on a judgment of overriding national interest. The fact that Japan has not yet ratified the nuclear nonproliferation treaty does not necessarily portend its rejection; it is rather an indication of Japanese prudence.

6

Attitudes Toward Remilitarization

Supporters of Remilitarization

The Japanese Right. The "right" in Japan can be described as an amorphous collection of organizations and individuals who harbor a wide variety of beliefs, professions, and personalities, including members of the ruling Liberal Democratic Party, ultra-rightist "patriotic" groups, religious associations, intellectuals, students, and even gangster bands. The Public Security Investigation Agency estimates a total of more than 400 registered rightist organizations with a membership of about 120,000, a reported increase of some 60 percent over the number existing in 1960. In addition there are said to be some 3,500 so-called "gangster" groups, boasting a membership of 140,000, who usually support rightist causes. Student groups with a rightist tinge have been estimated at about thirty with as many as 300,000 members. According to sources identified as rightist, sympathizers for these various organizations and causes may number more than 2.5 million.[1]

The political influence of the Japanese right cannot be judged in terms of numbers, however, but rather in the relationships which certain individuals may have with influential politicians. Thus, certain prominent members of the LDP maintain a variety of associations with right-wing groups and are said to be influenced by them. Rumors have circulated of connections, financial and otherwise, between politicians

---

[1] The figures are quoted from Koji Nakamura, "The Samurai Spirit," *Far Eastern Economic Review*, vol. 74, no. 42 (16 October 1971), p. 22; most were said to originate from the Public Security Investigation Agency, but those on "gangsters," student groups, and sympathizers may be exaggerated.

and unsavory underworld characters, and occasionally some scandal has burst into the public eye. Usually these relationships have remained below the surface.

In the 1970s the so-called "hard core" rightist organizations are seeking to bring about what they term the "Showa restoration." Taking the name of the present emperor's era, these groups aim to wipe out leftist opposition, glorify patriotism and nationalism, and strengthen military power. To achieve the last, their first goal is revision of Article 9 of the Constitution, the "no-war" clause. Other aims include the "establishment of an autonomous defense structure" (another way of proposing the acquisition of a nuclear capacity), securing the return of the northern islands from the Soviet Union (the only aim with wide popular appeal), and the nationalization of the Yasukuni Shrine (the shrine to war heroes, honored as a symbol of nationalism in the prewar period). Needless to say, most rightist groups favor complete rearmament, including conscription.

The ritual suicide in November 1970 of Mishima Yukio, one of Japan's most famous novelists and leader of a right-wing, para-military organization, dramatized his appeal to amend the Constitution, to replace the "illegitimate Self Defense Forces" with a "genuine" military force, and to restore the "true samurai spirit." Some observers feared that Mishima's exhortations, which failed to arouse the Self Defense Forces to action, would nevertheless inspire a resurgence of rightist sentiment and influence within the country. Although many Japanese were sobered by the incident and some youths committed, or tried to commit, *hara-kiri* in imitation of Mishima, little lasting effect was produced. A year after the event, Kawabata Yasunari, Nobel prize-winning novelist and friend of Mishima, who himself later committed suicide because of poor health, probably accurately appraised the impact of Mishima's act: "I do not think that his death has affected the thinking of those active in politics now." [2]

The announcement of President Nixon's intention to visit Peking and China's admission into the United Nations stimulated sharp attacks from the far right against the Japanese government's efforts to develop a rapprochement with the People's Republic of China, at the same time these events spurred a renewal of the traditional rightist support for the Nationalist Chinese government.

---

[2] Kawabata's statement quoted by Richard Halloran, "Japanese Honor Mishima a Year after His Death," *New York Times,* 26 November 1971, p. 15.

If the support of the right for remilitarization is not substantial in terms of votes and Japanese public opinion, its effect on members of the LDP, industrialists, and other influential individuals should not be ignored.

The Right Wing of the Liberal Democratic Party. Although a "right wing" is not precisely identifiable as an organized group within the LDP, unquestionably a number of LDP Diet members favor constitutional revision to free Japan from legal restrictions and political inhibitions against full and complete rearmament. Constitutional revision, including the amendment of Article 9, has been a plank in the party platform since the formation of the LDP in 1955; it has not, however, been a live issue in recent years because public opinion has consistently, and strongly, clung to the "no-war" clause. Kishi Nobusuke, a former prime minister and a leader in the so-called "right wing" of the party, has for many years championed revision of Article 9 and was reported in 1971 to be chairman of a "Dietmen's League for an Autonomous Constitution," which claimed a membership of more than a third of the members of both houses of the Diet (264 out of 741). A research council and subcommittees to study specific parts of the Constitution were established and, according to press reports, were expected to draft a general outline of a revised Constitution. The stated objective was to bring about constitutional revision during the decade of the 1970s, characterized by some Japanese as the last major postwar task of the LDP after the reversion of Okinawa.[3]

A movement for constitutional reform would become more influential if it could generate popular appeal. Few politicians, however, find either popularity or votes in campaigning against Article 9 or for the remilitarization of Japan. Changing circumstances, particularly a different international climate such as a marked relinquishment of defense responsibilities in Asia by the United States, could make constitutional revision a more politically profitable cause in the future. At the present time, however, with its popular majorities having diminished in recent elections and tough opposition ahead, the LDP is not likely soon to embrace the cause of constitutional revision, which would require a two-thirds vote in the Diet and a majority vote in a national referendum. Prime Minister Sato affirmed several times in the Diet during 1971 that he had no intention of revising the Constitution.

---

[3] *Nihon Keizai Shimbun,* 3 February 1971.

Individual Proponents of Remilitarization. The Japanese public is reminded from time to time that certain prominent citizens in influential positions believe that Japan should throw off the shackles of Article 9 and rearm openly and fully. The open expression of such opinions usually creates a sensation. The opposition parties and the press invariably find the public sympathetic to attacks on those who question Article 9, and they exploit each such incident to the limit.

In February 1968 Minister of Agriculture Kuraishi Tadao in an unguarded moment referred to "our silly Constitution" and compared Japan to "a kept woman dependent on foreigners." "By the Constitution," he said, "we must depend on the faith of others. . . . This is 'salvation by faith.' " [4] The furor in the Diet was so great—a boycott paralyzed business for seventeen days—that in spite of all explanations and apologies, the minister was forced to resign from the cabinet.

A second incident which aroused nationwide repercussions in 1969 occurred when the director of the Japan Federation of Employers Associations (*Nikkeiren*), Sakurada Takeshi, declared his support for the revision of Article 9. The press reported: "It came as a shock to the general public that he [Sakurada] stated that 'All the people of good sense want the Government to carry on the affairs of State courageously, and at the same time, think it is necessary for the nation to revise the Constitution. . . .' " [5] One of Sakurada's principal reasons for supporting revision was to permit Japan to "strengthen its own defense power."

Executives of companies producing military equipment have a special interest in a greater defense effort for Japan and some have expressed themselves openly on the subject. A few have publicly declared that Japan should become a nuclear power. The most prominent Japanese industrialists, however, have opposed remilitarization and the production of nuclear weapons. These include both the president and vice-president of the powerful Federation of Economic Organizations (*Keidanren*), Uemura Kogoro and Iwasa Yoshizane; the latter is also chairman of Japan's largest commercial bank, the Fuji Bank. Other businessmen who may favor revision of the Constitution have not expressed their opinions publicly. The sensation created by those who have done so gives a clue to the cause of their inhibitions. Still, the very powerful suggestions that remilitarization would only hinder Japan's

---

[4] *Mainichi Shimbun,* 7 February 1968.
[5] *Tokyo Shimbun,* 18 October 1969.

profitable economic advances into China, Southeast Asia, and other areas are probably convincing to a majority of Japanese industrial leaders.

To summarize, the men who would remove the restrictions imposed by the Constitution—that is, those who would permit Japan's military forces to assume missions which were broader than the strictly limited one of country defense, and who would support the production of nuclear weapons—are formed of rightist groups, certain elements within the Liberal Democratic Party, a few industrialists, and some individuals with special interests. At the present time these groups and individuals do not carry great weight in the total political spectrum. The development of their future influence will depend more upon events outside Japan than upon what happens within.

Opponents of Remilitarization

Political Parties. All four of Japan's major opposition political parties reject rearmament. All defend Article 9. As we have seen they differ somewhat in their positions on the Self Defense Forces and the security treaty with the United States. Only the Socialists preach unarmed neutrality; all others would maintain armed forces of one sort or another, even the Communists. All oppose the security treaty in its present form: the Socialist and Communist parties—and recently the Komeito—would abolish it outright, the Democratic Socialist Party would alter its character through revision. All opposition parties oppose increases in defense budgets and caution against the dangers of a revival of militarism. All refuse to consider any security commitments for Japan outside of defense of the home islands. Some argue for a treaty of friendship and nonaggression signed by China, the Soviet Union, the United States, and Japan.

While it is unlikely that the conservative monopoly of political power in Japan will soon be broken, the LDP percentage of the popular vote has been steadily shrinking. In the last elections the percentage of votes for LDP candidates for the House of Representatives (December 1972) was well below the halfway mark, 46.9 percent, as compared to 47.6 percent in the 1969 general election.[6] In the vote for upper house candidates in June 1971, the LDP share dropped to 44.4 percent in the national constituencies, as compared with 46.7 percent in the 1968

---

[6] Independents garnered about 5 percent of the vote in each of these elections.

elections. The four opposition parties together garnered 46.9 percent of the total vote in 1969, 49.6 percent in the national constituencies in 1971, and 47.9 percent in lower house elections in 1972. Thus, if this trend should continue and if these parties should ever be able to form a united front, they could unseat the LDP. Only the failure, thus far, of the leftists to forge a workable coalition on a national scale has saved the conservatives. With respect to defense, the opposition views are shared by many Japanese who regularly vote for LDP candidates.

Organizations. The peace movement in Japan, which is opposed to all forms of rearmament, consists of a multifarious aggregation of groups, alliances, and sometimes loosely connected entities, which are deeply divided between those affiliated with the Japan Communist Party and those opposed to it, the latter elements again fragmented into numerous units generally labeled the "New Left." The peace movement cannot be easily isolated from the so-called "reformist struggle," which brings under one umbrella students, youth, labor, antiwar marchers, and even the fringe of radical bomb throwers, deplored by most of the other reformists, especially by those under the aegis of the JCP.

The principal causes which inspire the activities of the left relate to security. From the time of the riots protesting revision of the U.S.-Japan security treaty in 1960, the history of Japan's reformist movement has been a succession of protests and demonstrations over defense issues. Marches and rallies were organized against the entry into Japanese ports of American nuclear-powered submarines, against the visit of the aircraft carrier *Enterprise,* against the maintenance of American military bases in Japan and Okinawa, against the continuation in force of the security treaty, against the stationing of B-52 planes in Okinawa, against the use of American bases in Japan and Okinawa for operations in the Vietnam War, against the construction of an international airport near Tokyo on the grounds that it would be utilized by military aircraft, and against the Okinawa reversion treaty because it permitted the United States to continue to maintain military bases in Okinawa. Only a few issues seized upon for protest by the leftists during recent years were not directly related to security; one was the treaty normalizing relations with the Republic of Korea signed in 1964, and even that agreement was believed by the government to be in the interest of Japan's security and was attacked by the left as the first step toward the formation of a military bloc, the so-called "NEATO."

Among organizations identified by slogans and rhetoric with the peace movement are the two councils against atomic and hydrogen bombs, *Gensuikyo* and *Gensuikin* (the JSP offshoot of *Gensuikyo*), the Citizen's League for Peace in Vietnam *(Beheiren)*, and the Antiwar Youth Committee *(Hansen Seinen Iinkai)*. The anti-A-and-H-bomb movement has been discussed in Chapter 1. *Beheiren* was founded in 1965 at the time of the bombing of North Vietnam as a loosely structured association without regular membership or a national organization. It suffered at the hands of the extremist youth groups, lost strength, and has since been disbanded. The Antiwar Youth Committee attempted to attract young factory workers and was originally controlled by the Socialist Party; Socialist influence diminished as more radical elements gained power within the organization.

The youth and student movements are more seriously split than ever. The membership of the pro-JCP Democratic Youth League is probably still largest, approximately 180,000 in 1972. The "New Left" embraces the Trotskyites and numerous splinter factions, all hostile to the JCP and to each other. More prominent in this spectrum than in previous years are the extreme radical groups such as the "Red Army" and the "United Red Army" which perpetrate bomb-throwing, theft, and assassination. Their slogan is: "Break out of the mass struggles of the '60s and raise the curtain on the armed struggles of the '70s." Thirty policemen were injured during 1971, and on 21 August the Red Army killed an officer of the Self Defense Forces. The United Red Army perpetrated executions of its own members in 1972 and was responsible for the Tel Aviv airport massacre in May 1972. Arrests of radical students rose in 1971 to 7,000 from 4,558 the previous year.

Mass demonstrations and "one-day joint struggles" by the Communist and Socialist parties brought occasions for the antiwar elements to take to the streets. In 1970 the cry was "smash the security treaty" and on 23 June, the day the treaty became subject to notice of termination, a record 774,000 people gathered in rallies across the country— some 200,000 more than the combined assemblies of 1960. The effect of the treaty demonstrations was, however, judged to have been "largely symbolic." [7] In 1971 and the early part of 1972 the left directed its attention toward Okinawa and the reversion agreement to be signed and ratified during 1972. One-day "general strikes" protesting the continued

---

[7] *New York Times,* 24 June 1970.

maintenance of American forces and bases in the Ryukyu Islands were held in Okinawa in both May and November 1971, and these set off sympathetic strikes and rallies in the main Japanese islands.

The three principal days of protest in 1971 were 28 April, "Okinawa Day" (the anniversary of the effective date of the San Francisco peace treaty which accorded temporary administration of Okinawa to the United States); 19 May, "Okinawa General Strike"; and 21 October, "International Antiwar Day." While the demonstrators were fewer in number than in the previous year, the rallies were marred by acts of violence. During an otherwise peaceful march in Okinawa on 10 November in connection with a general strike, a small group of extremist youths murdered an Okinawan policeman. Authorities disclosed later that the youths directly incited the crowd against the police. Their antiwar idealism had turned to hostility toward the guardians of the law. In 1972 several "one-day joint struggles" were sponsored as usual by the Socialist and Communist parties but they were peaceful demonstrations and created little disruption or popular impact.

By 1972 the character of the youth and student movements in Japan—as in the United States—had changed from mass action to isolated bombing attacks and assassinations, the latter directed at the police, and, in one instance, at the Self Defense Forces. This change in strategy and tactics had little to do with the essential antidefense character of the movement, which still prevailed. As for the country as a whole, President Nixon's visit to China, the parliamentary chaos over the defense budget, Prime Minister Tanaka's visit to Peking, and the recognition of the People's Republic of China all strengthened popular opposition to remilitarization. The arguments for security lost potency in the atmosphere of détente which pervaded the country.

Recent Public Opinion Polls

As we have seen, Japanese security is a frequent topic for public opinion surveys. Allowing for the varying nature of the issues which form the security problem, the influence of timing on the polls, and the effect of the phraseology of the questions asked, a certain consistency has appeared. To summarize, a study of the most recent polls suggests that most Japanese do not favor marked increases in the military establishment nor the acquisition or production by Japan of nuclear weapons; yet a respectable minority sees inevitable trends in this direction. As we

100

have seen, no serious sense of threat from any other nation emerges. The security treaty with the United States, no longer a burning issue since its automatic continuation from 1970, is regarded with skepticism and some anxiety, but public interest in it has obviously flagged. The idea that Japan might assume the military role of the United States in Asia finds little encouragement. Some Japanese clearly took the Chinese, Soviet and North Korean propaganda charges about a revival of militarism in Japan seriously and admitted that such revival was possible and dangerous for the future, but few agreed that militarism had already revived.

Polls in 1971 and 1972 reflected many of the same attitudes often expressed in the past. Some changes suggested a greater tolerance toward what was seen as an inevitable growth in Japan's military strength. The impression remained that the Japanese public opposed unrestricted rearmament for Japan in the sense of a large military establishment, offensive weapons, the ability to carry on military operations beyond the Japanese islands, and the possession of nuclear weapons. The polls indicated that the Japanese, at least for the time being, were still averse to choosing the road to military power.

Defense Capacity. The Japanese have been accused of being unable to chart a course of leadership for their nation, which is now the world's third largest industrial power. For the past few years, Japan's "role" has been the subject of innumerable books, articles, discussions, and debates. Much of the argument has centered around the question whether a nation can be a great power without possessing commensurate military power. Many Japanese leaders have said that Japan should prove to the world that it is possible. A poll published by the *Asahi* on 3 January 1972 illustrates this search for a destiny. The question was asked: "Which course do you think it is good for Japan to follow in the future?" A multiple choice was offered with the following results:

Direction	Percent
Economic big power	9
Welfare nation	53
Military big power	3
Leading position in international areas	3
Aid to developing nations and peaceful coexistence	20
Other answers	2
No answer	10

These results are consistent with attitudes revealed by responses on many related issues which show great reluctance to seek military power or responsibilities for security beyond the defense of the homeland.

Opinions regarding the expansion of military power or defense budgets have remained remarkably consistent. To a question asked by the government broadcasting system (NHK) in September 1971 as to whether Japan's defense effort was insufficient, 52.4 percent replied "no" against 22.5 percent "yes." To a similar poll which queried whether a policy to increase defense power was desirable, the answers were: "no," 40.4 percent; "yes," 10.3 percent; "inevitable," 34.3 percent; and "don't know," 15 percent.[8] In a July 1971 poll, more than 50 percent of the respondents stated that the defense budget proposed for the Fourth Defense Buildup Plan was excessive, 36.1 percent found it "suitable" and only 3.9 percent "too low." [9] In a poll taken more than a year and a half later, only 17.7 percent approved the level of the Fourth Defense Buildup Plan, 11.4 percent called for its reduction, 14.4 percent thought the amount inevitable but opposed the domestic production of armaments, and 35.7 percent supported total cancellation of the plan with the budget to be used for housing and welfare.[10]

Self Defense Forces. The Self Defense Forces have finally won the respect of the Japanese public and in recent years polls have shown that they are both accepted and supported. However, when an increase in the SDF is proposed, the reaction is still uniformly negative. In an April 1971 poll, more than half of the replies called the present strength of the SDF "satisfactory," 15 percent wanted a reduction, and 6.5 percent favored total dissolution. Only 22.2 percent favored an increase.[11] There has never been much doubt about Japanese attitudes toward compulsory military service. A poll published in June 1971 showed 78 percent of those queried opposed a revival of the conscription system; only 9 percent approved.[12]

Nuclear Weapons. Attitudes toward the possession by Japan of nuclear weapons have been consistently negative, although the "nuclear allergy" seems to be weakening. Asked in 1971 about the American nuclear

---

8 *Yomiuri Shimbun,* 19 October 1971.
9 *Sankei Shimbun,* 30 April 1971, published in *Yoron Chosa,* vol. 3 no. 7 (July 1971), p. 83.
10 *Tokyo Shimbun,* 24 November 1972.
11 *Sankei Shimbun,* 30 April 1971.
12 *Yoron Chosa,* vol. 3, no. 6 (June 1971), p. 73.

bombing of Hiroshima and Nagasaki, 43 percent believed it "inhumane and impermissable," but 52 percent judged it inhumane but no longer resented very strongly by them. Others described the bombing as "unavoidable for the United States," or labeled it natural as a war measure.[13] In another survey published the same month, 52 percent of the respondents considered nuclear weapons "not necessary," whereas only 7 percent thought they were. At the same time, the Japanese public shows confidence in the technological capacity of the country to produce weapons if required. An *Asahi* poll asked in December 1971: "Do you think Japan's industrial power can produce powerful weapons in large quantities at any time?" The results were "yes," 47 percent; "no," 27 percent; and "no answer," 23 percent.[14]

Consistent polling conducted in the Tokyo area by the Institute of Statistical Mathematics, Ministry of Education, on the subject of nuclear armament has shown that since 1968 a majority "opposes unequivocally" Japan's possession of nuclear weapons. The 1971 poll produced the highest figure for this group—59 percent—of any in a series of seven surveys. Those who thought that having nuclear weapons was "unavoidable under certain circumstances" formed sizable minorities varying between 30 and 40 percent. A telephone poll, taken by *Sankei* in the Tokyo and Osaka areas in December 1971, revealed similar uncertainty on the subject of whether Japan *would* acquire nuclear weapons—quite apart from their desirability. Asked whether Japan would have nuclear weapons within ten years, 44 percent replied affirmatively, 40 percent said "no." Gallup was asked to pose the same question in the United States at the same time. An overwhelming percentage of Americans (77) believed Japan would possess nuclear weapons within ten years; only 12 percent thought not.[15] A 1972 Japanese poll revealed increases both in those who believed Japan's possession of nuclear weapons to be "undesirable" (82.2 percent) and in those who thought Japan *would* have them in the future (51.7 percent). Only 10 percent thought them desirable, while 35.3 percent held that *Japan* would *not* acquire nuclear weapons.[16]

Security Treaty. Although other international issues have crowded the U.S.-Japan security treaty off the front pages of the newspapers since

---

[13] *Asahi Shimbun,* 3 June 1971.
[14] Ibid., 3 January 1972.
[15] *Sankei Shimbun,* 11 December 1972.
[16] *Yoron Chosa,* vol. 4, no. 10 (October 1972), p. 78.

the left failed to prevent its automatic extension in 1970, the public has continued to evidence awareness that the existence of the treaty has an influence on Japan's international position. For example, in June 1971 *Asahi* probed opinions on whether the security treaty was obstructing relations between Japan and China. Forty-six percent said "yes," while 20 percent answered "no" and 30 percent had no opinion.[17] In the same month another poll inquired into the best means for maintaining the peace and security of Japan. Various answers were suggested but no single solution received majority support. "Japanese-American cooperation under the security treaty" won 15 percent and the vague "security through the United Nations," 18 percent. The highest percentage went to "a policy of neutralism" (28 percent); only 11 percent believed Japan should "seek independence through a strengthening of the Self Defense Forces." [18]

The perennial argument over whether the United States will in fact defend Japan under the obligations of the security treaty has been repeatedly tested in numerous polls. In October 1971 *Yomiuri* asked: "Do you think that in case of emergency America will defend Japan under the U.S.-Japan security treaty?" The "nos" were 38.2 percent; the "yeses" 29.6; the "don't knows" 32.2 percent.[19] These results were less conclusive than those of a 1969 *Asahi* poll which had recorded 47 percent as believing that the United States would *not* defend Japan and 31 percent as thinking it would.[20] In December 1971 *Sankei* and Gallup simultaneously polled Japanese (in Tokyo and Osaka only) and Americans on the subject of whether the United States would aid Japan in case of a nuclear attack. Surprisingly, 51 percent of the Japanese polled believed American "armed assistance" would be forthcoming while only 12 percent thought the United States would "leave Japan alone." American opinion was quite different: 34 percent felt the United States would aid Japan but 47 percent thought it would not. The polls taken in the two countries were not strictly comparable and too definitive conclusions should not be drawn from the results. Other polls have shown the Japanese much more skeptical of the American response in the case of a nuclear attack on Japan. Yet in October 1972, 33 percent of

---

[17] *Asahi Shimbun,* 3 June 1971.
[18] *Yoron Chosa,* vol. 3, no. 6 (June 1971), pp. 72-74.
[19] *Yomiuri Shimbun,* 19 October 1971.
[20] *Asahi Shimbun,* 1 October 1969.

respondents to a poll in Japan favored maintaining the security treaty while 20.7 percent would scrap it.[21]

Japan and the U.S. Military Burden. The idea of Japan's assuming the American military burden in Asia is a subject of keen interest to both commentators and pollsters. *Yomiuri* asked in October 1971: "Do you worry that Japan might come to take over the United States role in Asia in the future?" Replies were almost equally divided: "yes," 38.6 percent; "no," 35.6 percent; and "don't know," 30.7 percent.[22] An *Asahi* poll published in January 1972 put the query differently: "There is the view that since the Self Defense Forces exist to defend Japan they can take over the burden of American forces in Asia. Do you think so?" Fifty-six percent replied "no," 20 percent stated they "do *not* think they *cannot*"[23] take over the burden and 24 percent either gave other answers (4 percent) or had no answer (20 percent).[24]

Revival of Militarism. As was discussed in Chapter 3, the Japanese seem fascinated by arguments over a possible revival of Japanese militarism. Their fascination originated from a war-guilt complex which has been stimulated not only by the campaigns of the opposition parties, but even more by the barrage of Chinese, Soviet, and even American charges which have been hurled at them. Numerous surveys in 1971 investigated this question. The polls were fairly consistent in continuing to show that only small percentages of respondents believed that militarism *had already* revived. A good many were ready to admit that militarism might be reviving, that there was danger of its reviving, or that there was a possibility of its reviving. In October 1971, *Yomiuri* found 42.5 percent who agreed that militarism "is reviving," while only 7.3 percent would conclude that it "had revived."[25] An NHK poll in September revealed 38 percent as feeling that militarism was reviving "to some extent" or that there was a danger it would revive in the future.[26] In a January 1972 poll, the *Tokyo Shimbun* asked the direct question: "Do you think militarism is reviving in Japan?" The uncertainty of the respondents was indicated by their answers: "yes," 30.3

---

[21] *Yoron Chosa*, vol. 4, no. 12 (December 1972), p. 83.
[22] *Yomiuri Shimbun*, 19 October 1971.
[23] The direct translation of the double negative conveys the nuance of uncertainty common to many Japanese expressions, including replies to polls.
[24] *Asahi Shimbun*, 3 January 1972.
[25] *Yomiuri Shimbun*, 19 October 1971.
[26] NHK poll, 26, 27, 28 September 1971.

percent; "no," 29.8 percent; "cannot say which," 25.1 percent; "don't know," 15 percent.[27]

Attitudes of Youth. Some observers have speculated that a younger generation without wartime experience would be more nationalistic and would seek military power as a future goal. While in any country youthful attitudes are traditionally believed to change with maturity, the younger Japanese generation shows little sign at present of cherishing military power as a future national objective. For example, a 1970 poll at Tokyo University showed that opinions about defense capability, nuclear weapons and military alliances were far more negative among students than among the general public. Seventy-six percent of the Tokyo students opposed the possession of nuclear weapons, as contrasted with only 45 percent for the public at large; moreover, 50 percent of the students rejected any strengthening of defense power, while among adults, the figure was only 11 percent. The students were against military pacts with either Communist or non-Communist nations, 48 percent in the former case, 62 percent in the latter.[28]

Despite inconsistencies and inaccuracies in individual surveys— as we have seen, these are implicit in Japanese polls—on questions related to defense, there is sufficient corroboration among varying questions to draw a general conclusion. Summarized, this is that the Japanese lack ambition for a military role and do not favor or welcome remilitarization, including the possession and production of nuclear weapons (see Appendix, Document 14). But some take a fatalistic attitude, not uncommon in their culture, that there are certain inevitable trends which it is hopeless to resist.

---

[27] *Tokyo Shimbun* (evening edition), 4 January 1972.
[28] *Yomiuri Shimbun,* 19 June 1970.

7
Will Japan Rearm?

Sources of Attitudes

Decision making in Japan is a complex process, not easily separated into identifiable steps, and neither precise nor determined by rule. The Liberal Democratic Party and government reach a consensus on major issues, taking into consideration the attitudes and opinions of many groups and forces, including those of the opposition. National defense, of course, is a major issue affecting both domestic and foreign affairs. To draw conclusions from "Japanese attitudes" about this issue we must ascertain the sources of attitudes and judge their respective weights in the final determination of national policy. First comes the party itself.

The Liberal Democratic Party. The LDP, whose power to form governments seems assured for the foreseeable future, chooses the prime minister who in turn selects his cabinet. The government can indeed be viewed as the creature of the party, and it is usually party policy that determines government policy. Members of the government are often graduates of the bureaucracy (in contrast to the situation in the United States where so many politicians come from the legal profession), and thus the influence of the ministries and their permanent personnel is brought heavily to bear on the decision-making machinery of the government. The bureaucracies of certain ministries, such as Finance and Trade and Industry, exert powerful influences which fundamentally affect the determination of national policy.

Party policy on defense has been quite consistent. Except for the fringes, where attitudes of the one extreme favor all-out rearmament including nuclear weapons and those of the other support further arms restrictions or reductions, the party's mainstream has supported a policy of gradually augmented, balanced, conventional defense, taking into consideration the new obligation to defend Okinawa and the effect of further reductions in American military strength in both Japan and Okinawa. This attitude is described as "defensive defense," a phrase popular in Diet discussions. It does not include revision of the Constitution to remove Article 9, conscription, or the possession or production of nuclear weapons.

The Industrialists. The Japanese system could with some justification be termed a "government-industrial complex" because of the close relationship between leaders of industry and leaders of government and the bureaucracy. Defense is of special interest because of the stimulus to military production and the possible development of a defense industry. Apart from the special interests of the defense industrialists, the Japanese *zaikai* are generally conservative in orientation and support national defense. But they do not necessarily advocate remilitarization, and they exhibit no desire to return to the status of the prewar *zaibatsu* with the entangling ties which, in essence, subordinated them to a powerful military. Most are keenly conscious of the priority requirement for maximum trade opportunities around the world, and they see a remilitarized Japan as an obstacle to profitable economic expansion, particularly in China and Southeast Asia. *Zaikai* attitudes, if one is to generalize, favor a respectable military establishment under a policy of gradually augmented, conventional self-defense, but one safely under control. Some, of course, may wish for unfettered rearmament but prefer not to speak out.

The Opposition Political Parties. So long as the LDP maintains a comfortable working majority in both houses of the Diet, no opposition party and no coalition of parties can threaten its dominance. When necessary, the LDP can always force legislation through, as it did in the case of the revision of the security treaty in 1960, the normalization treaty with the Republic of Korea in 1965, and the Okinawa reversion treaty in 1971. This would not be possible for constitutional revision, which requires a two-thirds vote, a larger majority than the LDP now possesses in either house.

The prime minister wishes to avoid boycott disruption of the Diet and charges of creating and using a "tyranny of the majority." Consequently the LDP leadership tolerates the arguments of the opposition and tailors its strategy accordingly. The prime minister and responsible cabinet ministers respond to prolonged, persistent, and hostile questions from Socialist and Communist members, often directed to relations with the United States and to defense policy. In certain instances, especially when boycott has been threatened or instituted, the LDP has bowed to the opposition. We have already referred to the 1968 resignation of the minister of agriculture under fire in the Diet for an offhand remark to the press on Japan's lack of adequate defense. One of the successive directors-general of the Defense Agency, Nishimura Naomi, resigned in 1971 because of the storm of opposition protest over a comment considered derogatory to the United Nations. A more recent example was the resignation in May 1973 of JDA Director-General Masuhara Keikichi over a press conference in which Masuhara discussed his briefing of the emperor on defense matters.[1] Thus far no prime minister has ever thought it politically feasible to propose in the Diet that the Defense Agency be upgraded to a ministry. The disturbance provoked by such an action would, in the view of the LDP, outweigh the advantages of added prestige for the Self Defense Forces.

Opposition attitudes do not change basic policy, but they may affect its implementation. The Socialist and Communist parties know that they can spark demonstrations outside the Diet to match the trouble which their representatives will cause within, and the government is sensitive to this threat. The gingerly way in which the government handled the visits of American nuclear-powered submarines is a case in point. It took most scrupulous care in scheduling and arranging visits, with the closest cooperation and coordination maintained at all times between the foreign office and the American embassy. In short, the opposition—despite its minority position—ever holds the threat not only of disrupting parliamentary proceedings, but of seriously weakening the majority party's ability to govern. Confronted with the new strength of the Communist party as a result of the 1972 elections, the government leadership must be even more prudent in handling the opposition. Tanaka's steps to confer with leaders of the other political parties show his recognition of their potential for obstruction.

---

[1] See Richard Halloran, "Japan's Leftists Hobbling Tanaka," *New York Times,* 2 June 1973.

The Military. Unlike the military of any other major nation in the modern world, Japanese men in uniform play little part in the determination of national policy, even in matters directly related to defense. Their first disability is that the defense establishment is relegated within the government to the secondary status of an agency. In addition, the Defense Agency itself is thoroughly civilian and its is partially staffed by bureaucrats on loan from more powerful ministries that retain their loyalties. Subject to constant critical surveillance from the opposition and the press, who delight in exposing any sign of irregularity in the SDF, the officers of the armed services lead restricted, almost completely nonpolitical lives. There is little opportunity for direct military input into the decision-making process above the third or fourth echelon of the government bureaucracy. Realizing the unpopularity of defense issues and understanding the adverse political effects of strong advocacy, even the ruling party, which provides the SDF with its primary support, will compromise on the defense issue before any other. Neither the opposition nor the LDP has any interest in increasing the political voice of the military in Japan. As a consequence, whatever decision the Japanese may make on vital foreign affairs or defense issues will be made without significant influence from the uniformed leaders of the SDF.

Mass Communications Media. Japan is saturated with the printed and spoken word. Newspapers cover the country; their total circulation is third largest in the world, after the United States and the Soviet Union: one newspaper is printed for every two persons. Over 90 percent of Japanese households own television sets and are served by nearly 3,000 stations operating in all parts of the country. Book publishing is also third largest in the world. Many newspapers are organs of political parties or special interest groups; others are strictly commercial. The government operates a national radio network, NHK, which broadcasts no advertising. The three principal Tokyo dailies (*Asahi, Mainichi,* and *Yomiuri*) are simultaneously available throughout Japan; their editorial policies have been biased in one direction or another but they carry a wide variety of national and international news with editorialists and columnists who frequently disagree among themselves. With these facilities, the attitudes and opinions of government officials, politicians, scholars, businessmen and representatives of all professions and walks of life are thoroughly disseminated.

Japanese newspapers have traditionally been antigovernment in content and many of them continue to be. The media express the whole spectrum of opinion, with even government radio and television programming commentaries by Communists, Socialists and numerous forceful critics of the national administration. Yet on the defense question one can accurately conclude that the preponderance of editorial comment opposes the remilitarization of Japan, the acquisition of nuclear weapons and the assumption by Japan of a security role in Asia.

Elections. Presumably the best measures of the ultimate effect of public opinion on policy in a democracy are the results of elections. In terms of measure, Japanese voters, by returning LDP majorities in consecutive elections, have consistently endorsed the foreign policies of the government, including that on defense. It must be added though that the choice of Japanese voters is dictated more by the political appeal and local strength of individual candidates than by foreign policy or defense issues. Of most immediate concern to the average voter are day-to-day problems such as prices, taxes, environment, health, education, and welfare.

Conclusions

These are the conclusions to which our analysis of Japanese attitudes leads:

(1) Japan will not remilitarize in the sense of returning to the predominant military system of prewar Japan. Except for a small rightwing fringe which has existed ever since the war, few if any Japanese seek any semblance of prewar militarism for their nation.

(2) Japan will improve the quality and quantity of her conventional armaments in this decade, both by developing her defense industry and by judicious importation of arms from abroad.

(3) It is unlikely that Japan will decide in the foreseeable future to produce nuclear weapons.

(4) Japan and the United States will continue to maintain their mutual security treaty for at least the next few years.

It is true that the security treaty presents something of a dilemma for the Japanese. Many of them accept it as a cheap insurance policy which is better to keep than to cancel. Yet the idea of "autonomous defense" is in the air, and economic capacity makes such an objective

111

conceivable. The question is whether the treaty is compatible with that concept; the government claims that it is. True autonomy in defense, however, presupposes termination of the treaty. It also raises the alternative specters of a Japan defenseless in the face of a nuclear threat, or a Japan nuclear-armed in the name of "autonomous defense." Neither course appears popular in Japan at present.

Rapprochement with China has affected Japanese attitudes toward defense as well as toward the security treaty. Now that diplomatic relations have been established with the People's Republic, the Japanese leadership and the public must logically perceive a diminished threat from mainland China. Furthermore, although the security treaty was long believed to be a serious obstacle to improved Sino-Japanese relations, this has proved not to be the case. Not only was the treaty not an obstacle to normalization, but Chou En-lai has let it be known that he does not now object to maintenance of Japanese defense forces nor to the treaty itself. While such an attitude may change, the security treaty has for the moment ceased to be an issue in relations between Japan and the People's Republic of China.

Recent events in East Asia have stimulated a mood in Japan that a relaxation of tensions has indeed occurred. Beginning with President Nixon's steps to open a new relationship with the People's Republic of China and to progress toward strategic arms agreements with the Soviet Union, the year 1972 saw not only Japan's diplomatic recognition of the PRC but also the moves of North and South Korea in the direction of eventual reunification. The culmination of this series of events—the agreement on a cease-fire in Indochina in early 1973—was welcomed in Japan with enormous relief. In the light of these international developments, the Japanese exhibit less anxiety over the security of Korea, less concern over the dangers to them of American military intervention in Asia and—assuming the status quo or peaceful change in Taiwan—less fear from China. This does not mean that the LDP leadership feels assured that "peace has broken out" to the extent that vigilance and defense potential are no longer necessary. Open hostilities between China and the Soviet Union, a breakdown in the Korean truce with resumed warfare, or—remote as it may seem—a Chinese decision to "liberate" Taiwan could shatter Japanese complacency. However, in Japan a "mood" can be a potent force, and any feeling of threat that has existed in the past has been perceptibly reduced.

Considering the détente atmosphere of early 1973, there is little likelihood that in the foreseeable future Japan will choose remilitarization, including the production of nuclear weapons. No prime minister, subject as he is to a party consensus, would think of adopting that course. Yet, while Prime Minister Tanaka will continue to have difficulty in obtaining the defense appropriations his government recommends, the Japanese can be expected generally to support the steady but moderate growth projected in their future defense planning.

Appendix

DOCUMENT 1: PREAMBLE AND ARTICLE 9 FROM
THE CONSTITUTION OF JAPAN
Promulgated 3 November 1946

Preamble

We, the Japanese people, acting through our duly elected representatives in the National Diet, determined that we shall secure for ourselves and our posterity the fruits of peaceful cooperation with all nations and the blessings of liberty throughout this land, and resolved that never again shall we be visited with the horrors of war through the action of government, do proclaim that sovereign power resides with the people and do firmly establish this Constitution. Government is a sacred trust of the people, the authority for which is derived from the people, the powers of which are exercised by the representatives of the people, and the benefits of which are enjoyed by the people. This is a universal principle of mankind upon which this Constitution is founded. We reject and revoke all constitutions, laws, ordinances, and rescripts in conflict herewith.

We, the Japanese people, desire peace for all time and are deeply conscious of the high ideals controlling human relationship, and we have determined to preserve our security and existence, trusting in the justice and faith of the peace-loving peoples of the world. We desire to occupy an honored place in an international society striving for the preservation of peace, and the banishment of tyranny and slavery, oppression and intolerance for all time from the earth. We recognize that all peoples of the world have the right to live in peace, free from fear and want.

We believe that no nation is responsible to itself alone, but that laws of political morality are universal; and that obedience to such laws is incumbent upon all nations who would sustain their own sovereignty and justify their sovereign relationship with other nations.

We, the Japanese people, pledge our national honor to accomplish these high ideals and purposes with all our resources.

*   *   *

115

Chapter II—Renunciation of War

Article 9. Aspiring sincerely to an international peace based on justice and order, the Japanese people forever renounce war as a sovereign right of the nation and the threat or use of force as means of settling international disputes.

In order to accomplish the aim of the preceding paragraph, land, sea, and air forces, as well as other war potential, will never be maintained. The right of belligerency of the state will not be recognized.

DOCUMENT 2: EXCERPTS FROM THE ALLIED TREATY OF
PEACE WITH JAPAN
8 September 1951

Whereas the Allied Powers and Japan are resolved that henceforth their relations shall be those of nations which, as sovereign equals, cooperate in friendly association to promote their common welfare and to maintain international peace and security, and are therefore desirous of concluding a Treaty of Peace which will settle questions still outstanding as a result of the existence of a state of war between them;

Whereas Japan for its part declares its intention to apply for membership in the United Nations and in all circumstances to conform to the principles of the Charter of the United Nations; to strive to realize the objectives of the Universal Declaration of Human Rights; to seek to create within Japan conditions of stability and well-being as defined in Articles 55 and 56 of the Charter of the United Nations and already initiated by post-surrender Japanese legislation; and in public and private trade and commerce to conform to internationally accepted fair practices;

Whereas the Allied Powers welcome the intentions of Japan set out in the foregoing paragraph;

The Allied Powers and Japan have therefore determined to conclude the present Treaty of Peace, and have accordingly appointed the undersigned Plenipotentiaries, who, after presentation of their full powers, found in good and due form, have agreed on the following provisions:

Chapter I—Peace

Article 1. (a) The state of war between Japan and each of the Allied Powers is terminated as from the date on which the present Treaty comes into force between Japan and the Allied Power concerned as provided for in Article 23.

(b) The Allied Powers recognize the full sovereignty of the Japanese people over Japan and its territorial waters.

* * *

Chapter III—Security

Article 5. (a) Japan accepts the obligations set forth in Article 2 of the Charter of the United Nations, and in particular the obligations

(i) to settle its international disputes by peaceful means in such a manner that international peace and security, and justice, are not endangered;

(ii) to refrain in its international relations from the threat or use of force against the territorial integrity or political independence of any State or in any other manner inconsistent with the Purposes of the United Nations;

(iii) to give the United Nations every assistance in any action it takes in accordance with the Charter and to refrain from giving assistance to any State against which the United Nations may take preventive or enforcement action.

(b) The Allied Powers confirm that they will be guided by the principles of Article 2 of the Charter of the United Nations in their relations with Japan.

(c) The Allied Powers for their part recognize that Japan as a sovereign nation possesses the inherent right of individual or collective self-defense referred to in Article 51 of the Charter of the United Nations and that Japan may voluntarily enter into collective security arrangements.

Article 6. (a) All occupation forces of the Allied Powers shall be withdrawn from Japan as soon as possible after the coming into force of the present Treaty, and in any case not later than 90 days thereafter. Nothing in this provision shall, however, prevent the stationing or retention of foreign armed forces in Japanese territory under or in consequence of any bilateral or multilateral agreements which have been or may be made between one or more of the Allied Powers, on the one hand, and Japan on the other.

DOCUMENT 3: EXCERPTS FROM THE MUTUAL DEFENSE ASSISTANCE AGREEMENT BETWEEN JAPAN AND THE UNITED STATES
8 March 1954

The Government of Japan and the Government of the United States of America:

Desiring to foster international peace and security, within the framework of the Charter of the United Nations, through voluntary arrangements which will further the ability of nations dedicated to the purposes and principles of the Charter to develop effective measures for individual and collective self-defense in support of those purposes and principles;

Reaffirming their belief as stated in the Treaty of Peace with Japan signed at the city of San Francisco on September 8, 1951 that Japan as a sovereign nation possesses the inherent right of individual or collective self-defense referred to in Article 51 of the Charter of the United Nations;

Recalling the preamble of the Security Treaty between Japan and the United States of America, signed at the city of San Francisco on September 8, 1951, to the effect that the United States of America, in the interest of peace and security, would maintain certain of its armed forces in and about Japan as a provisional arrangement in the expectation that Japan will itself increasingly assume responsibility for its own defense against direct and indirect aggression, always avoiding any armament which could be an offensive threat or serve other than to promote peace and security in accordance with the purposes and principles of the Charter of the United Nations;

Recognizing that, in the planning of a defense assistance program for Japan, economic stability will be an essential element for consideration in the development of its defense capacities, and that Japan can contribute only to the extent permitted by its general economic condition and capacities;

Taking into consideration the support that the Government of the United States of America has brought to these principles by enacting the Mutual Defense Assistance Act of 1949, as amended, and the Mutual Security Act of 1951, as amended, which provide for the furnishing of defense assistance by the United States of America in furtherance of the objectives referred to above; and

Desiring to set forth the conditions which will govern the furnishing of such assistance;

Have agreed as follows:

Article I

1. Each Government, consistently with the principle that economic stability is essential to international peace and security, will make available to the other and to such other governments as the two Governments signatory to the present Agreement may in each case agree upon, such equipment, materials, services, or other assistance as the Government furnishing such assistance may authorize, in accordance with such detailed arrangements as may be made between them. The furnishing and use of any such assistance as may be authorized by either Government shall be consistent with the Charter of the United Nations. Such assistance as may be made available by the Government of the United States of America pursuant to the present Agreement will be furnished under those provisions, and subject to all of those terms, conditions and termination provisions of the Mutual Defense Assistance Act of 1949, the Mutual Security Act of 1951, acts amendatory and supplementary thereto and appropriation acts thereunder which may affect the furnishing of such assistance.

* * *

Article VIII

The Government of Japan, reaffirming its determination to join in promoting international understanding and good will, and maintaining world peace, to take such action as may be mutually agreed upon to eliminate causes of international tension, and to fulfill the military obligations which the Government of Japan has assumed under the Security Treaty between Japan and the United States of America, will make, consistent with the political and economic stability of Japan, the full contribution permitted by its manpower, resources, facilities and general economic condition to the development and maintenance of its own defensive strength and the defensive strength of the free world, take all reasonable measures which may be needed to develop its defense capacities, and take appropriate steps to ensure the effective utilization of any assistance provided by the Government of the United States of America.

Article IX

1. Nothing contained in the present Agreement shall be construed to alter or otherwise modify the Security Treaty between Japan and the United States of America or any arrangements concluded thereunder.

2. The present Agreement will be implemented by each Government in accordance with the constitutional provisions of the respective countries.

DOCUMENT 4: THE TREATY OF MUTUAL COOPERATION AND SECURITY BETWEEN THE UNITED STATES AND JAPAN (1960 Revision)

The United States of America and Japan,

Desiring to strengthen the bonds of peace and friendship traditionally existing between them, and to uphold the principles of democracy, individual liberty, and the rule of law,

Desiring further to encourage closer economic cooperation between them and to promote conditions of economic stability and well-being in their countries,

Reaffirming their faith in the purposes and principles of the Charter of the United Nations, and their desire to live in peace with all peoples and all governments,

Recognizing that they have the inherent right of individual or collective self-defense as affirmed in the Charter of the United Nations,

Considering that they have a common concern in the maintenance of international peace and security in the Far East,

Having resolved to conclude a treaty of mutual cooperation and security,

Therefore agree as follows:

Article I

The Parties undertake, as set forth in the Charter of the United Nations, to settle any international disputes in which they may be involved by peaceful means in such a manner that international peace and security and justice are not endangered and to refrain in their international relations from the threat or use of force against the territorial integrity or political independence of any state, or in any other manner inconsistent with the purposes of the United Nations.

The Parties will endeavor in concert with other peace-loving countries to strengthen the United Nations so that its mission of maintaining international peace and security may be discharged more effectively.

Article II

The Parties will contribute toward the further development of peaceful and friendly international relations by strengthening their free institutions, by bringing about a better understanding of the principles upon which these institutions are founded, and by promoting conditions of stability and well being. They will seek to eliminate conflict in their international economic policies and will encourage economic collaboration between them.

Article III

The Parties, individually and in cooperation with each other, by means of continuous and effective self-help and mutual aid will maintain and develop, subject to their constitutional provisions, their capacities to resist armed attack.

Article IV

The Parties will consult together from time to time regarding the implementation of this Treaty, and, at the request of either Party, whenever the security of Japan or international peace and security in the Far East is threatened.

Article V

Each Party recognizes that an armed attack against either Party in the territories under the administration of Japan would be dangerous to its own peace and safety and declares that it would act to meet the common danger in accordance with its constitutional provisions and processes.

Any such armed attack and all measures taken as a result thereof shall be immediately reported to the Security Council of the United Nations in accordance with the provisions of Article 51 of the Charter. Such measures shall be terminated when the Security Council has taken the measures necessary to restore and maintain international peace and security.

Article VI

For the purpose of contributing to the security of Japan and the maintenance of international peace and security in the Far East, the United States of America is granted the use by its land, air and naval forces of facilities and areas in Japan.

The use of these facilities and areas as well as the status of United States armed forces in Japan shall be governed by a separate agreement, replacing the Administrative Agreement under Article III of the Security Treaty between the United States of America and Japan, signed at Tokyo on February 28, 1952, as amended, and by such other arrangements as may be agreed upon.

Article VII

This Treaty does not affect and shall not be interpreted as affecting in any way the rights and obligations of the Parties under the Charter of the United Nations or the responsibility of the United Nations for the maintenance of international peace and security.

Article VIII

This Treaty shall be ratified by the United States of America and Japan in accordance with their respective constitutional processes and will enter into force on the date on which the instruments of ratification thereof have been exchanged by them in Tokyo.

Article IX

The Security Treaty between the United States of America and Japan signed at the city of San Francisco on September 8, 1951 shall expire upon the entering into force of this Treaty.

Article X

This Treaty shall remain in force until in the opinion of the Governments of the United States of America and Japan there shall have come into force such United Nations arrangements as will satisfactorily provide for the maintenance of international peace and security in the Japan area.

However, after the Treaty has been in force for ten years, either Party may give notice to the other Party of its intention to terminate the Treaty, in which case the Treaty shall terminate one year after such notice has been given.

In witness whereof the undersigned Plenipotentiaries have signed this Treaty.

Done in duplicate at Washington in the English and Japanese languages, both equally authentic, this 19th day of January, 1960.

For the United States of America:

Christian A. Herter

Douglas MacArthur II

For Japan:

Nobusuke Kishi

Aiichiro Fujiyama

DOCUMENT 5: THE EXCHANGE OF NOTES
INCORPORATING AGREED CONSULTATION FORMULA

Japanese Note

Excellency:

I have the honour to refer to the Treaty of Mutual Cooperation and Security between Japan and the United States of America signed today, and to inform Your Excellency that the following is the understanding of the Government of Japan concerning the implementation of Article VI thereof:

> Major changes in the deployment into Japan of United States armed forces, major changes in their equipment, and the use of facilities and areas in Japan as bases for military combat operations to be undertaken from Japan other than those conducted under Article V of the said Treaty, shall be the subjects of prior consultation with the Government of Japan.

I should be appreciative if Your Excellency would confirm on behalf of your Government that this is also the understanding of the Government of the United States of America.

I avail myself of this opportunity to renew to Your Excellency the assurance of my highest consideration.

U.S. Reply

Excellency:

I have the honor to acknowledge the receipt of Your Excellency's Note of today's date, which reads as follows:

[Text of note]

I have the honor to confirm on behalf of my Government that the foregoing is also the understanding of the Government of the United States of America.

Accept, Excellency, the renewed assurances of my highest consideration.

Washington, January 19, 1960.

DOCUMENT 6: EXCERPT FROM THE JOINT STATEMENT BY PRESIDENT JOHNSON AND PRIME MINISTER SATO
15 November 1967

V

The President and the Prime Minister exchanged views frankly on the matter of security in the Far East including Japan. They declared it to be the fundamental policy of both countries to maintain firmly the Treaty of Mutual Cooperation and Security between the United States and Japan in order to ensure the security of Japan and the peace and security of the Far East. The President and the Prime Minister recognized that maintenance of peace and security rests not only upon military factors, but also upon political stability and economic development. The Prime Minister stated that Japan is prepared to make a positive contribution to the peace and stability of Asia in accordance with its capabilities. The President stated that such efforts on the part of Japan would be a highly valued contribution.

DOCUMENT 7: EXCERPTS FROM THE JOINT COMMUNIQUE BETWEEN PRESIDENT NIXON AND PRIME MINISTER SATO
21 November 1969

III

The President and the Prime Minister exchanged frank views on the current international situation, with particular attention to developments in the Far East.

The President, while emphasizing that the countries in the area were expected to make their own efforts for the stability of the area, gave assurance that the United States would continue to contribute to the maintenance of international peace and security in the Far East by honoring its defense treaty obligation in the area.

The Prime Minister, appreciating the determination of the United States, stressed that it was important for the peace and security of the Far East that the United States should be in a position to carry out fully its obligations referred to by the President.

He further expressed his recognition that, in the light of the present situation, the presence of United States forces in the Far East constituted a mainstay for the stability of the area.

IV

The President and the Prime Minister specifically noted the continuing tension over the Korean peninsula. The Prime Minister deeply appreciated the peacekeeping efforts of the United Nations in the area and stated that the security of the Republic of Korea was essential to Japan's own security.

The President and the Prime Minister shared the hope that Communist China would adopt a more cooperative and constructive attitude in its external relations.

The President referred to the treaty obligations of his country to the Republic of China which the United States would uphold. The Prime Minister said that the maintenance of peace and security in the Taiwan area was also a most important factor for the security of Japan.

The President described the earnest efforts made by the United States for a peaceful and just settlement of the Vietnam problem.

The President and the Prime Minister expressed the strong hope that the war in Vietnam would be concluded before the return of the administrative rights over Okinawa to Japan.

In this connection, they agreed that, should peace in Vietnam not have been realized by the time reversion of Okinawa is scheduled to take place, the two governments would fully consult with each other in the light of the situation at that time so that reversion would be accomplished without affecting the United States efforts to assure the South Vietnamese people the opportunity to determine their own political future without outside interference.

The Prime Minister stated that Japan was exploring what role she could play in bringing about stability in the Indo-China area.

V

In light of the current situation and the prospects in the Far East, the President and the Prime Minister agreed that they highly valued the role played by the Treaty of Mutual Cooperation and Security in maintaining the peace and security of the Far East including Japan, and they affirmed the intention of the two governments firmly to maintain the Treaty on the basis of mutual trust and common evaluation of the international situation.

They further agreed that the two governments should maintain close contact with each other on matters affecting the peace and security of the Far East including Japan, and on the implementation of the Treaty of Mutual Cooperation and Security.

VI

The Prime Minister emphasized his view that the time had come to respond to the strong desire of the people of Japan, of both the mainland and Okinawa, to have the administrative rights over Okinawa returned to Japan on the basis of the friendly relations between the United States and Japan and thereby to restore Okinawa to its normal status.

The President expressed appreciation of the Prime Minister's view. The President and the Prime Minister also recognized the vital role played by United States forces in Okinawa in the present situation in the Far East. As a result of their discussion, it was agreed that the mutual security interests of the United States and Japan could be accommodated within arrangements for the return of the administrative rights over Okinawa to Japan.

They therefore agreed that the two governments would immediately enter into consultations regarding specific arrangements for accomplishing the early reversion of Okinawa without detriment to the security of the Far East including Japan.

They further agreed to expedite the consultations with a view to accomplishing the reversion during 1972 subject to the conclusion of these specific arrangements with the necessary legislative support.

In this connection, the Prime Minister made clear the intention of his government, following reversion, to assume gradually the responsibility for the immediate defense of Okinawa as part of Japan's defense efforts for her own territories.

The President and the Prime Minister agreed also that the United States would retain under the terms of the Treaty of Mutual Cooperation and Security such military facilities and areas in Okinawa as required in the mutual security of both countries.

VII

The President and the Prime Minister agreed that upon return of the administrative rights, the Treaty of Mutual Cooperation and Security and its related arrangements would apply to Okinawa without modification thereof.

In this connection, the Prime Minister affirmed the recognition of his government that the security of Japan could not be adequately maintained without international peace and security in the Far East and therefore, the security of countries in the Far East was a matter of serious concern for Japan.

The Prime Minister was of the view that, in the light of such recognition on the part of the Japanese Government, the return of the administrative rights over Okinawa in the manner agreed above should not hinder the effective discharge of the international obligations assumed by the United States for the defense of countries in the Far East including Japan. The President replied that he shared the Prime Minister's view.

VIII

The Prime Minister described in detail the particular sentiment of the Japanese people against nuclear weapons and the policy of the Japanese Government reflecting such sentiment.

The President expressed his deep understanding and assured the Prime Minister that, without prejudice to the position of the United States Government with respect to the prior consultation system under the Treaty of Mutual Cooperation and Security, the reversion of Okinawa would be carried out in a manner consistent with the policy of the Japanese Government as described by the Prime Minister.

DOCUMENT 8: EXCERPTS FROM PRESIDENT NIXON'S 1970 REPORT TO CONGRESS, "UNITED STATES FOREIGN POLICY FOR THE 1970's: A NEW STRATEGY FOR PEACE" 18 February 1970

Asia and the Pacific

Economic and Political Partnership. Japan, as one of the great industrial nations of the world, has a unique and essential role to play in the development of the new Asia. Our policy toward Japan during the past year demonstrates our conception of the creative partnership we seek with all Asian nations.

Upon entering office, I faced a pivotal question concerning the future of our relations with Japan: the status of Okinawa. What did we consider more important—the maintenance of American administration of Okinawa with no adjustments in the conditions under which we operate our bases, or the strengthening of our relationship with Japan over the long term? We chose the second course because our cooperation with Japan will be crucial to our efforts to help other Asian nations develop in peace. Japan's partnership with us will be a key to the success of the Nixon Doctrine in Asia.

In November, I therefore agreed with Prime Minister Sato during his visit to Washington that we would proceed with arrangements for the return of Okinawa in 1972, with our bases remaining after its reversion in the same status as our bases in Japan. This was among the most important decisions I have taken as President.

For his part, Prime Minister Sato expressed the intention of the Japanese Government to expand and improve its aid programs in Asia in keeping with the economic growth of Japan. He agreed with me that attention to the economic needs of the developing countries was essential to the development of international peace and stability. He stated Japan's intention to accelerate the reduction and removal of its restrictions on trade and capital. He also stated that Japan was exploring what it could do to help bring about stability and reconstruction in postwar Southeast Asia. The Prime Minister affirmed that it is in Japan's interest that we carry out fully our defensive commitments in East Asia.

We have thereby laid the foundation for U.S.-Japanese cooperation in the 1970s.

                         *   *   *

Issues for the Future. The fostering of self-reliance is the new purpose
and direction of American involvement in Asia. But we are only at
the beginning of a new road. However clear our conception of where
we wish to go, we must be under no illusion that any policy can provide easy answers to the hard, specific issues which will confront us
in Asia in coming years.

                         *   *   *

A sound relationship with Japan is crucial in our common effort
to secure peace, security, and a rising living standard in the Pacific area.
We look forward to extending the cooperative relationship we deepened
in 1969. But we shall not ask Japan to assume responsibilities inconsistent with the deeply felt concerns of its people.

DOCUMENT 9: EXCERPTS FROM "THE DEFENSE OF JAPAN"
ISSUED BY THE JAPAN DEFENSE AGENCY, TOKYO
20 October 1970

* * *

Part II—Way for Japan's Defense

* * *

2. Basis of National Defense

The basis of our country's national defense is determined by the Constitution of Japan, by laws and ordinances, and by policies concerning national defense, formulated on the basis of the Constitution. Our country has as its goal the construction of a peace state, a cultural nation and a welfare state, based on freedom and democracy. Our country's national defense policies must be considered within the context of this goal. Furthermore, in the light of the fact that modern national defense must harmonize its military and nonmilitary aspects, defense policies must be given the correct relationship to the nation's other policies.

(1) The Constitution and Japan's Defense
The right of self-defense is an inherent right which a nation naturally possesses, as long as it is a sovereign, independent state. It is natural that it has the right to exercise it.

Our country's Constitution provides that "war as a sovereign right of the nation and the threat or use of force as the means of settling international disputes will be forever renounced." However, in case the nation suffers an armed attack from the outside, it does not renounce the right to exercise armed force in order to eliminate such attacks in self-defense. To block armed attack, when the nation suffers such armed attack from another country, is precisely self-defense, and it is essentially different in nature from the settlement of international disputes. The Constitution does not prohibit the use of armed force as a means of defending our country, in the case of armed attack. It is natural for an independent nation to exercise its right of self-defense when it suffers an armed attack from another country, and to eliminate it.

It is also a matter of course for our country to have self-defense power for exercising this inherent right of self-defense.

As our country's defense power is for self-defense, its scale must be such as is proper and necessary for self-defense. This kind of defense power does not constitute war potential, the possession of which is prohibited by the Constitution.

The so-called Sunakawa Judgment of the Supreme Court, handed down on 16 December 1959, states as follows, in regard to the interpretation of the Constitution:

> It does not, in any way, deny the inherent right of self-defense, which our country has as a sovereign state, and the pacifism of our country's Constitution definitely does not prescribe non-defense and nonresistance. . . . That our country can take measures for self-defense necessary for maintaining our country's peace and security and for ensuring its survival must be said to be natural, as the exercise of functions inherent to a state.

It thus recognizes that self-defense measures can be taken in order to counter armed attacks.

*   *   *

3. Japan's Defense Power

(1) Autonomous Defense and the United States-Japan Security System
Prime Minister Sato explained at a recent session of the Diet that "autonomous defense means that each person has the spirit of independence, and that the defense of the nation will be provided primarily by the people themselves." This is a statement that national defense is primarily a question of the people's mental attitude. National defense is the task of the people, to be carried out by the people as a whole, a task which cannot be accomplished without rallying together the power of all the people. The most important thing, furthermore, is the will for defense, or the will to defend the peace and independence of our country to the last. In other words, this is patriotism. It is not an exaggeration to say that, without such a spiritual foundation, a nation's defense cannot be assured.

To defend the nation's independence and peace ourselves is natural for an independent nation, and all nations are making efforts toward this end. Our country is also making autonomous defense efforts, commensurate with the increase in our country's economic power and the rise in our country's international position. In other words, our country

135

has set up a basic policy for coping with aggression primarily by its own power and is continuing efforts to establish a system which will enable it effectively to carry out a defense which is exclusively defensive.

However, today, in this nuclear age, it is extremely difficult for any nation to ensure perfect defense for the nation alone. Just as many other nations are adopting collective security systems, our country also has a system for deterring aggression from the outside by a security arrangement with the United States, with which it shares many interests in politics, economies and other fields, and we will cope with external aggression through this arrangement. This is a system under which Japan aims to ensure perfect defense for herself with our country's own defense power together with the military power of the United States, based on the United States-Japan security treaty. So long as we do not have nuclear weapons and other offensive weapons, the United States-Japan security treaty will be necessary for Japan's security, assuming there are no major changes in the international situation.

A collective security system is a joint defense, standing on the basis of the nation's independent nature, and it is not contradictory to autonomous defense. In society today, autonomous defense does not necessarily mean single-handed defense. If it is in cooperation with other nations for the defense of national interests, while ensuring its own autonomy, a collective security system is also one form of autonomous defense. However, one point to which we should pay attention in considering joint defense is that the nation must not harbor vague expectations from the other side, or fall into dependence on, or seek to be saved by the other partner. Such expectations and dependence will implant a sense of irresponsibility toward national defense among the people, which contains the danger of demoralizing the national spirit. It will also lower the partner's confidence in our country, and there is the danger that it will weaken Japan's defense and its security arrangement based on mutual cooperation. It is necessary to establish an autonomous defense setup with the aim of defending our own country by ourselves, and to develop the road to effective mutual cooperation, backed by national consensus.

*　*　*

(4) Defense Power Adhering Strictly to Defense
The basic principle for our country's defense power is that it should adhere strictly and exclusively to defense.

Defense power adhering strictly and exclusively to defense means that, in case of aggression against our country, Japan will adhere completely to a strategic defensive position through the invocation of the inherent right to self-defense. Consequently, all such questions as the amount of defense power, the quality of the defense force such as with what weapons they will be equipped, and the form action should take in coping with aggression, will be limited to the scope of self-defense. In other words, defense strictly and exclusively for defense is in consonance with that which the Constitution allows for the defense of the homeland.

Standing on the foregoing premise, our country sets as its goal the consolidation of defense power through use of conventional weapons capable of coping effectively with limited wars.

Many of the armed disputes which can be expected to arise in international society today will be limited wars. This fact is clearly indicated by the armed disputes which have occurred in various places, since the end of World War II. The usual way to prevent or cope with armed disputes using conventional weapons is to counter with conventional weapons. This is the reason why conventional weapons still continue to be regarded with importance, even after the development of nuclear weapons.

Consideration of international reactions and awareness of the possibility that a limited war could escalate into a large-scale war, like World War II prevent the use of even tactical nuclear weapons, let alone strategic nuclear weapons.

(5) Limits of Defense Power

a. Constitutional Limits

(a) Since our country's defense power is for self-defense, its scale must naturally be that which is proper and necessary for self-defense. What degree of defense power this means in concrete terms cannot be stated categorically, because of varying conditions, such as the circumstances and the development of science and technology at a given time. However, it is possible to say, at any rate, that Japan cannot possess weapons which will pose a threat of aggression to other nations, such as long-range bombers like B52s, offensive aircraft carriers and ICBMs, for example.

(b) Also, as our country's defense power is for self-defense, it cannot take action which exceeds the scope of self-defense. In other words, the deployment of the Self Defense Forces will be ordered when there is direct or indirect aggression against our country; consequently, there would be no question of overseas dispatch of forces.

b. Limitation from the Standpoint of Policy

(a) As regards nuclear weapons, we adopt the three nonnuclear principles. If small nuclear weapons are within the scale of real power needed for the minimum necessary limit for self-defense, and if they are such as not to constitute a threat of aggression toward other nations, one can say that possession thereof is possible, in a legal sense. However, the Government adopts the policy of not having nuclear equipment as its policy even if this is possible from the standpoint of the Constitution.

(b) Our country will gradually consolidate efficient defense power corresponding to our country's national ability and national circumstances, within the necessary limit for self-defense, and in keeping with other policies, such as those for social security and education. Consequently, in regard to the allocation of state resources for the consolidation of defense power, it is not necessarily proper to determine the amount in simple proportion to the increase and growth of its economic power or by its percentage of the gross national product or national budget.

Based on the above, the scale, content and pace of the consolidation of our country's defense power will be determined. There are, therefore, strict limitations, peculiar to our country.

* * *

4. Japan-United States Security Arrangements

* * *

(2) Japan's Defense Based on United States-Japan Security Treaty

In article 5 of the security treaty, Japan and the United States stipulate that "an armed attack against either party in areas under the administration of Japan will be recognized as endangering the peace and security of their respective nations," and that they will cope with it as a common danger.

The United States bears the obligation to defend Japan. Our country, however, does not bear an obligation to defend United States forces, even if they are attacked, if they are in United States territory or areas other than our country's territory. This is a form different from that taken in the United States-Republic of Korea Mutual Defense Assistance Treaty or the United States-Republic of China Mutual Defense Treaty, in which the Republic of Korea and the Republic of China adopt the policy of mutual defense with the United States toward armed attacks against either party in the Pacific or the Western Pacific area.

As already stated, the basic principle of our country's defense is strictly and exclusively defensive, and it is our policy to rely on United States in areas where our defense is inadequate. It goes without saying that the degrees of dependence on the United States for Japan's defense will differ, depending on the form of the armed attack or aggression against our country, its scale, and the length of time it takes to deal with it, and also according to the status of consolidation of our own defense power. However, generally speaking, it will be a deterrent against the threat of war using nuclear weapons, large-scale armed clashes and strategic attacks against areas outside our country's territory by direct aggression. At any rate, in the case of armed attacks our country, Japan and the United States must cope with them in the most effective way. Therefore, it is necessary for the two sides to be in close communication with each other, to work for an exchange of views, and to maintain close relations in normal times.

(3) Providing Areas and Facilities

Under Article 6 of the Treaty, the United States is accorded the right for its ground, naval and air forces to use facilities and areas in Japan, "to contribute to the security of Japan and to contribute to the maintenance of international peace and security in the Far East." This is based on the judgment that this is necessary in order to make the actions of the United States forces for the defense of Japan truly effective under the United States-Japan Security Treaty arrangement and also that the presence of the United States forces in our country will deter disputes from arising.

Also, the security of the Far East and the security of Japan are very closely related. Japan and the United States are both interested in maintaining peace and security in the Far East. The fact that United States forces preserve a setup for the maintenance of the security of the Far East, using the facilities and areas in our country, has the effect of deterring the rise of armed disputes in the Far East, and this, at the same time, contributes to the security of our counry.

Part III. Present State and Various Problems of Self Defense Forces

*   *   *

2. Features of the Self Defense Forces

(1) Civilian Control

It is an ironclad rule in democratic nations that politics controls military affairs. One lesson we must never forget in looking back at the past is the relationship of politics to military affairs and of diplomacy to military affairs in prewar days.

DOCUMENT 10: EXCERPTS FROM PRESIDENT NIXON'S 1971 REPORT TO CONGRESS, "UNITED STATES FOREIGN POLICY FOR THE 1970's: BUILDING FOR PEACE"
25 February 1971

Japan

Japan's economic growth is unprecedented. It has made her the third greatest economic power on earth. However, Japanese living standards still rank below those of many other developed countries, and there is a strong feeling in Japan that these standards must be raised— and raised rapidly.

Japan's wealth gives her a tremendous stake in the peace and stability of Asia, and the dynamism of her economy inevitably has a major impact on the entire region. In recognition of these facts, Japan has taken a major role in the regional activities of the area. As a permanent method of meeting her interests and discharging her responsibilities, however, these regional activities may not prove adequate. Moreover, Japan's position as a major beneficiary of a liberal international economic system is not consistent with her slowness in removing the restrictions which limit the access of others to her own vibrant domestic economy.

My Administration shares with the Government of Japan the conviction that our relationship is vital to the kind of world we both want. We are determined to act accordingly. But the future will require adjustments in the U.S.-Japanese relationship, and the issues involved are too important and their solutions too complicated to be viewed with any complacency on either side.

Fortunately, they are not. Both the Japanese and the American Governments regard each other with profound goodwill and mutual respect. Both are determined to show the greatest possible understanding of the interest of the other. The maintenance of that spirit of cooperation and goodwill is not only the goal of our policy toward Japan. It is also the best assurance that the policy will succeed.

In recognition of our growing interdependence and Japan's own increased stature, Prime Minister Sato and I agreed in November 1969 to enter into negotiations for the return of Okinawa to Japanese administration by 1972. I can now report that negotiations on this question, including the retention of our Okinawa bases, are progressing steadily.

Our aim is to reach the specific agreements this spring, allowing us to obtain the necessary legislative support to proceed with reversion in 1972.

Last December, we and the Japanese agreed to significant realignments in our military bases in Japan, which will result in a reduction of some 12,000 U.S. military personnel over the next several months without adversely affecting our ability to meet our commitments to Japan or other Asian allies. The Japanese have announced plans for continuing qualitative improvements of their own self-defense capabilities, enabling them to provide for substantially all of their conventional defense requirements.

The United States and Japan have everything to gain from a further expansion of already close and profitable economic ties. Japan has for many years been America's largest overseas customer, and I am pleased to report that in 1970 our exports to Japan grew by some 35% to approximately $4.5 billion. This included more than $1 billion worth of products from America's farms, equivalent to the production of 10 million acres and the labor of more than 100,000 farmers. American purchases from Japan are even larger. The United States takes some 27% of Japan's exports, amounting in 1970 to almost $5.9 billion. I am glad to note that Japan has accelerated its program of liberalizing its restrictions on imports, and is also easing its restrictions on foreign capital investment. Despite the barriers Japan still maintains, direct American investment in Japan presently amounts to more than $1 billion. I expect this figure will increase as recognition grows within Japan that its own self-interest lies in providing wider investment opportunities.

The friendly competitive relationship, which properly characterizes this greatest transoceanic commerce in the history of mankind, is not without difficulties. An example is the protracted negotiations over the question of Japan's textile exports to the U.S., but I am confident we can find a solution which will be in our mutual interest.

In the important area of foreign aid, cooperation rather than competition is the watchword. Japan announced during the year that it intended by 1975 to raise its foreign assistance contribution to one percent of its GNP. We anticipate Japan will take a leading role in international and regional aid efforts, hopefully with less emphasis on commercial financing than in the past.

We are two strong nations of different heritages and similar goals. If we can manage our extensive relationship effectively and imaginatively, it cannot help but contribute significantly to the well-being and prosperity of our two peoples and to the nations of the entire Pacific Basin.

DOCUMENT 11: EXCERPTS FROM THE JOINT STATEMENT BY PRIME MINISTER SATO AND PRESIDENT NIXON
7 January 1972

II

The Prime Minister and the President recognized that in the changing world situation today, there are hopeful trends pointing toward a relaxation of tension, and they emphasized the need for further efforts to encourage such trends so as to promote lasting peace and stability. These efforts would involve close cooperation between the two Governments and with other governments.

They also recognized that the maintenance of cooperative relations between Japan and the United States is an indispensable factor for peace and stability in Asia, and accordingly they confirmed that the two Governments would continue to consult closely on their respective Asian policies.

III

The Prime Minister and the President, recalling the more than 100 years of association between the two countries, emphasized the importance of U.S.-Japanese relations being founded on mutual trust and interdependence. In this connection, they highly valued the important role played by the Treaty of Mutual Cooperation and Security between Japan and the United States.

IV

The Prime Minister and the President discussed the problems relating to the return of Okinawa as contemplated in the joint communiqué of November 21, 1969. They were gratified that the reversion agreement signed on June 17, 1971, had received the support of the respective legislatures, and decided to effect the return of Okinawa to Japan on May 15, 1972.

The President indicated the intention of the United States Government to confirm upon reversion that the assurances of the United States Government concerning nuclear weapons on Okinawa have been fully carried out. To this the Prime Minister expressed his deep appreciation.

The Prime Minister explained to the President why he felt it necessary that, after reversion, the facilities and areas of the United States armed forces located in Okinawa be realigned or reduced to the extent possible, particularly those in areas densely populated or closely related to the industrial development. The President replied that these factors would be taken fully into consideration in working out after reversion mutually acceptable adjustments in the facilities and areas consistent with the purpose of the Treaty of Mutual Cooperation and Security.

DOCUMENT 12: EXCERPTS FROM PRESIDENT NIXON'S
1972 REPORT TO CONGRESS, "UNITED STATES FOREIGN
POLICY FOR THE 1970's: THE EMERGING
STRUCTURE OF PEACE"
9 February 1972

Japan

I

My Administration shares with the Government of Japan the conviction that our relationship is vital to the kind of world we both want. We are determined to act accordingly. But the future will require adjustments in the U.S.-Japanese relationship, and the issues involved are too important and their solutions too complicated to be viewed with any complacency on either side.

> U.S. Foreign Policy for the 1970's
> Report to the Congress
> February 25, 1971

Japan is our most important ally in Asia. It is our second greatest trading partner. It is an essential participant, if a stable world peace is to be built. Our security, our prosperity, and our global policies are therefore intimately and inextricably linked to the U.S.-Japanese relationship. The well-being of both countries requires cooperation and a shared commitment to the same fundamental goals.

Last year was critical for our relationship. It was a year both of stress and of progress. It brought a sharp awareness of the divergence of some of our interests—and in its wake, a better understanding of the need for the mature and equitable management of those divergences.

Our China and economic initiatives were a shock to the U.S.-Japanese relationship. Both grew out of the new realities of a changed world situation. For precisely that reason, they had an unsettling effect upon Japan, which had become accustomed to a U.S.-Japanese relationship rooted in the postwar period and based on a bipolar concept of world power. That relationship, however, had already been overtaken by time and Japan's phenomenal economic growth. The shocks of 1971, therefore, only accelerated an evolution in U.S.-Japanese relations that was in any event, overdue, unavoidable, and in the long run, desirable.

The U.S.-Japanese relationship is in the process of inevitable change, not because the alliance of the past decades has failed, but because it has succeeded.

—Asian stability was bolstered by our pledge to work together in the common defense. Our defense postures together provided the fabric of Japan's security, while our forward basing in the area contributed to regional defense.

—Asian development was symbolized by Japan's economic resurgence and encouraged by our fruitful economic links. As Japan gained in strength, our parallel development assistance efforts nourished a broader regional advance.

—Asian political freedoms were strengthened by the process of Japan's recovery under a democratic system of government. The health of political ties between our democracies served as an example to the democratic experiment elsewhere in Asia.

This relationship stands out as a major success of American post-war diplomacy. Its purpose was to provide the sustenance and security which Japan required for economic and psychological recovery from the trauma of World War II. That recovery is complete.

In a remarkable display of disciplined energy, the Japanese people have again placed their nation firmly in the front rank of international powers. Our relationship now requires greater reciprocity.

Japan's history reinforces the inevitability of this change. For it testifies eloquently to Japan's national pride and capacity to respond to changing conditions in its external surroundings. As an island power, Japan's participation in broad regional or global alliances has traditionally been limited and intermittent. As its recovery proceeded, it was certain that Japan would play a more autonomous role in world affairs. In retrospect, the last two decades will be seen as a transitional period in which Japan, while relying on U.S. economic support and military protection, reestablished its inner cohesion as a society, and defined a more independent national role for itself. That is as it should be.

By 1969, the cumulative strains imposed on the U.S.-Japanese relationship were considerable and evident.

—We needed to face the political and psychological implications of Japan's growing strength and pride. The Japanese island of Okinawa had been under American administration for more than 25 years. Okinawa's status would disrupt and embitter the U.S.-Japanese friendship unless it were changed to reflect the new realities.

—We needed to adjust our economic relations to reflect the fact that Japan had become the world's third greatest industrial power. Japan provided the largest overseas market for American goods as well as formidable competition to us in both our domestic and world markets. Japan also benefited greatly from the liberal trade policies of the United States. But Japan's insistence on restricting its own markets contributed to a growing imbalance in our trade, and was an anachronism, inconsistent with its economic strength and symbolizing a lack of economic reciprocity which could not be long sustained.

—We both needed to bring into better balance our contributions to Asian development. Japan's political cohesion and economic prowess gave it the capacity to make a major contribution— and its commerce and investments in Asia gave Japan a clear interest in the region's stability.

—Signs that China was moving toward more constructive contacts with other nations would impel the issue of China policy to the fore for both countries. Eventually, we would have to face the problem of harmonizing our changing national perspectives towards China.

—Japan had long since acquired the industrial and technological strength to assume responsibility for its own conventional defense. However, Japan continued to rely on American nuclear power for strategic security. It was, moreover, prevented by constitutional, political, and psychological factors, and by the attitudes of its Asian neighbors, from projecting military power beyond its own borders. Thus the Mutual Security Treaty continued to serve Japan's interests, as well as our own. Still it was clear that changes would come in our defense relationship as Japan regained its strength and pride.

We faced, then, not a desire for change but the dynamics of change. The question was not whether to maintain the partnership which had served us both so well. The question was how to inject into our relationship the characteristics of equality and reciprocity without which it could not be sustained.

We began with Okinawa. In November 1969, I met with Prime Minister Sato and we agreed on the broad principles which should govern the reversion of Okinawa to Japanese administration. The problems were many and difficult. Our military installations on Okinawa were central to the security shield which we helped provide to the free nations of East Asia, including Japan. The quarter-century of American administration had created a web of political and economic problems to resolve before reversion. But in 1971, our negotiations resulted in a treaty which terminated this last administrative vestige of the Second World War. We retain our military installations in Okinawa, but on the same basis as those in the Japanese home islands. Early this year, at Prime Minister Sato's request I agreed to speed up the final reversion. Thus, our recognition of Japan's needs for political self-assertion has enabled us to remove this long-standing irritant in our friendship.

Japan now plays a major and steadily increasing role in assisting other Asian nations with their development needs. After years of U.S. leadership in this field we greatly welcome Japan's increasing contribution—which reflects Japan's realization that its own interests require it to participate in shaping the environment of Asia. Japan has pledged one percent of its gross national product to assisting less developed countries. That goal is already being approached, although we would hope to see a greater Japanese use of grants and concessional loans rather than commercial credits. The Japanese are playing a particularly prominent role in the Asian Development Bank and in the international groupings providing assistance to Indonesia and the Philippines.

Japan is developing plans to strengthen its conventional defense capabilities over the next few years. This is a reflection of heightened Japanese self-reliance and readiness to assume greater responsibilities. This welcome trend has been accompanied by a consolidation of our own military facilities and a reduction of our forces in both Japan and Okinawa.

There has, therefore, been steady progress in recent years in the assumption by Japan of a role in world affairs more consistent with its power. However, there has been less progress in reshaping our bilateral relations along more reciprocal lines. Until this year, the Japanese still tended to consider that their dependence upon us limited independent political initiatives of our own, while their political problems commended some independence of initiative on their part. Similarly, in our

149

economic relationship, it was evident that Japan, like our European allies, tended to take our commitment to a liberal trading system for granted without extending equivalent access to its own market.

Both these attitudes were understandable. But both stood in the way of the necessary task of creating a more mature basis for the continuation of U.S.-Japanese cooperation. In 1971, both also proved to be incorrect.

I knew that the July 15 announcement of my forthcoming visit to Peking would have a profound impact on Japan. It brought China policy and Japan's own future role in a changing Asia abruptly to the forefront of our relationship. The issue of China policy is, if anything, even more important for Japan than for the United States. Geography, culture, history, and trade potential make it a central issue in Japanese domestic politics as well as a key aspect of Japan's foreign policy. On a matter of such intrinsic importance, Japan could not fail to be disturbed at any implication that our policies, which had been so closely aligned, were diverging.

It was also clear, however, that we shared a fundamental interest in improved relations with China. We both have an enormous stake in ending the era of confrontation in Asia. Japan is already China's largest trading associate, and for some time has had not only economic ties but trade representation in the People's Republic of China.

The issue between us, then, is not whether the opening to China is desirable—but the need to harmonize our sometimes differing perspectives and interests in a common strategic conception and a shared over-all goal.

For our part, we have made it clear that our aim in Peking is to establish a better mutual understanding of one another's policies. We will not seek or discuss bilateral arrangements that could adversely affect the interests of our allies. We have no interest in arrangements which would sacrifice our friendship with a long-standing ally to the need for better communication with a long-standing adversary.

Therefore, there is no cause for either Japan or the United States to feel a lack of trust concerning our parallel policies toward China. In the chapter of this report concerning China we have set forth the reasons why it was impossible for us to consult with our allies prior to the public announcement of the Peking visit. We have since that time consulted very widely. We have made particular efforts to assure Japan of the basic harmony which clearly exists between a lessening of Asian tensions and the health of the U.S.-Japanese friendship.

My recent meeting with Prime Minister Sato at San Clemente permitted the full review of our policies and purposes and was an integral part of my preparation for the talks in Peking.

We are not on a divergent course, and autonomous policies need not create strains in our relationship so long as we both recognize the need to mesh those policies. Both the autonomy and the basic harmony of our actions are implicit and essential elements in the new relationship of equality and reciprocity which we seek with Japan. We are not involved—and must not become involved—in a competitive race toward accommodation. But in a changing world, we are both concerned with the removal of old animosities. Our alliance must now serve as the firm foundation of a stable Asia upon which both of us can confidently seek a more balanced and productive relationship with our adversaries.

* * *

Last year therefore dramatized for both Japan and the United States the two truths which must be recognized if our relationship is to continue to prosper. We have a need to adjust our relationship—and we have the ability to do it in a way that serves the interests of both of our countries. The future health of our friendship is not served by ignoring our differences. Nor is it served by expectations that either country will subordinate its interests in order to maintain an atmosphere of perfect amity. The continuity of our relationship is too important to both of us to permit such a concentration on its atmosphere rather than its substance.

We recognize that some of our actions during the past year placed the Japanese Government in a difficult position. We recognize that our actions have accelerated the Japanese trend toward more autonomous policies. We regret the former, but could not do otherwise. We welcome the latter as both inevitable and desirable—inevitable because it reflects the reality of Japanese strength in the 1970's—desirable because it is a necessary step in the transformation of our relationship to the more mature and reciprocal partnership required in the 1970's.

We intend that Japan shall remain our most important Asian ally. We expect that the future will bring an even greater degree of interdependence between us. We believe the vitality of our friendship and our cooperation in international matters is essential to the stable Asia we both require—and to the peaceful world we both seek.

These are the convictions which led me to travel to Alaska to welcome to American soil the Emperor and Empress of Japan on the first visit abroad of a reigning Japanese monarch. These are the convictions which underlie the extensive and unique network of official contacts which we have established between Japanese Government officials and our own. For example, in September we had a joint meeting in Washington of seven Japanese Cabinet officers and their American counterparts, for a very wide-ranging and authoritative examination of our relationship.

It was to ensure the harmony of our policies that Prime Minister Sato and I met in San Clemente in January. We reviewed all aspects of the events of the previous year, and examined the tasks which lie before us. I stressed that the adjustments we seek in our relationship demonstrate our recognition of Japan's new status—not doubts about the value of our alliance. On their part, Prime Minister Sato and his colleagues left me confident that they, too, consider a sound political relationship between us as essential to Japanese interests and to our shared goals in Asia and the world.

The process of adjustment will sometimes be arduous. But in 1971 we proved that it can be done by making the necessary adjustments in several of the most important issues on our agenda. The unjustified complacency of the recent past has been replaced with a greater awareness of the task which we both face. That fact constitutes a solid basis for renewed confidence in the future of U.S.-Japanese cooperation, with all that such cooperation promises for the mutual benefit of our two peoples, and for the world's hopes for a stable structure of peace and prosperity.

DOCUMENT 13: COMPARISON OF DEFENSE EXPENDITURES AND MILITARY MANPOWER VARIOUS COUNTRIES
1970-1971 and 1971-1972

	Defense Expenditures					
	US$ millions		Per capita		Percentage of GNP	
	(1971)	(1972)	(1970)	(1971)	(1970)	(1971)
U.S.	78,743	83,400	373	378	7.8	7.3
U.S.S.R.	55,000	–	222	–	11.0	–
China (P.R.C.)[a]	8,000	–	–	–	–	–
United Kingdom	6,108	6,900	107	109	4.9	4.7
West Germany	5,961	7,568	104	100	3.3	2.8
France	5,202	6,241	118	101	4.0	3.1
Italy	2,651	3,244	48	49	2.8	2.6
Poland	2,350	–	68	70	5.2	5.2
East Germany	2,124	2,240	116	123	5.9	5.9
Czechoslovakia	1,875	–	122	127	5.8	5.8
Japan	1,864	2,600	16	18	0.8	0.7

Manpower—Total Regular Armed Forces		
	1970-1971	1971-1972
U.S.S.R.	3,305,000	3,375,000
China (P.R.C.)[a]	2,880,000	2,880,000
U.S.	3,066,000	2,699,000
India	980,000	960,000
South Korea (R.O.K.)	634,250	634,750
China (Taiwan)	540,000	500,000
South Vietnam	500,000	503,000
North Vietnam	492,000	513,250
North Korea (D.P.R.K.)	401,000	402,500
Pakistan	392,000	395,000
Indonesia	319,000	317,000
Japan	259,000	260,000

[a] Figures for China (P.R.C.) are estimates only.

Source: *The Military Balance, 1971-72* and *1972-73* (London: International Institute for Strategic Studies, 1971 and 1972).

153

Question 11. It will be one-fourth of a century since the promulgation of the Constitution. It is said that "the spirit of the Constitution has taken firm root among the people." Do you also think so, or do you not think so?

Think so 40%

Do not think so 47

Others; no answer 13

Question 12. Do you think that the Japanese government is upholding this Constitution, or do you think it is not doing so?

It is upholding it generally 38%

Upholding it in some points 45

Is hardly ever upholding it 8

Others; no answer 9

Question 13. Article 11 of the Constitution guarantees the people's basic human rights. As a practical question, do you think human rights are actually being respected?

Fully respected 5%

Respected 34

Not respected very much 50

Not respected at all 4

Others; no answer 7

Question 14. In Article 9 of the Constitution, it is prescribed that Japan renounces war as a means for settling international disputes and that Japan will not possess ground, sea, or air war potential. Do you think the present Self Defense Forces (SDF) are a violation of the Constitution, or do you not think so?

Violation of the Constitution 39%

Not a violation 45

Others; no answer 16

154

Question 17. We now wish to ask you questions about the Sino-U.S. summit talks held on the occasion of U.S. President Nixon's visit to China.

(a) As a result of the talks, what do you think has happened to international tension?

Tension decreased on an overall basis	4%
Tension decreased partially	43
Tension increased partially	14
Tension increased on an overall basis	5
Tension completely remains unchanged	19
Others; no answer	15

(b) It is a matter of course to be friendly with all nations, but for Japan's foreign policy in the future, on which of the following do you think emphasis should be placed?

To continue cooperation with U.S.	12%
To make more efforts than in the past for cooperation with China	20
To endeavor more than in the past for cooperation with the U.S.S.R.	2
To maintain equal distance with U.S., China and U.S.S.R.	55
Others; no answer	11

Question 18. When you compare your actual feelings in regard to China with the government's policy toward China, which of the following applies to your situation?

There is very great difference	22%
There is some amount of difference	46
There is not much difference	15
There is no difference at all	2
Others; no answer	15

Question 19. We will next ask you what your impressions regarding the People's Republic of China (Peking) are.

(a) Do you receive the impression of "brightness" or an impression of "gloominess"?

Bright	44%
Gloomy	45
Others; no answer	11

(b) Do you receive the impression of "warmth" or an impression that it is "cold"?

Warm 40%
Cold 47
Others; no answer 13

Question 20. Japan has concluded the U.S.-Japan Security Treaty with the U.S. Do you think that this U.S.-Japanese Security Treaty is helpful or not helpful for the security of Japan?

Helpful 48%
Not helpful 25
Dangerous 14
Others; no answer 13

Question 21. There is the view, in regard to this U.S.-Japan Security Treaty, that "now that the Sino-U.S. talks have also been held, its meaning has lessened." Do you think this is true or not?

Think it is true 38%
Do not think it is true 47
Others; no answer 15

Question 23. Have you ever felt some uneasiness or displeasure because of the presence of U.S. military bases?

Feel it strongly 19%
Feel it to some degree 43
Do not feel it very much 27
Never felt it at all 6
Others; no answer 5

Question 24. Do you think that U.S. bases in Japan should be decreased in the future, in the light of President Nixon's visit to China, et cetera, or do you not think so?

Should be completely abolished 23%
Should be decreased gradually 55
Should watch the situation, without decreasing them
    at the moment 14
Must absolutely not be decreased 1
Others; no answer 7

Question 25. All opposition parties are showing a more negative attitude than the LDP toward the U.S.-Japan Security Treaty, the SDF and their dispatch to Okinawa, although there are some differences in nuances among the opposition parties. Do you think that these opposition attitudes are based on full consideration of the security of Japan?

Fully consider Japan's security 31%
Not considering it very much 54
Others; no answer 15

Question 26. (a) Do you think that the danger of Japan's (including Okinawa) being attacked by other countries or its being directly embroiled in war may possibly arise in the near future, or do you think that there will probably not arise such a danger?

Likely to arise 4%
May perhaps arise 43
Not likely to arise 39
Will absolutely not arise 8
Others; no answer 6

(b) Do you think there may arise a danger of internal uprisings in Japan, in the near future, with the assistance of funds from other nations, or under foreign countries' ideological influence?

Likely to arise 3%
May perhaps arise 31
Not likely to arise 46
Will absolutely not arise 12
Others; no answer 8

Question 27. Do you think or do you not think that Japan should have nuclear armaments?

Should arm itself with nuclear armaments immediately   2%
Should arm itself with nuclear armaments in the near
    future 11
Should do so sometime or other 22
Should absolutely not arm itself with nuclear weapons   58
Others; no answer 7

Question 28. Japan's defense expenditures correspond to 0.9 percent of its GNP. With the growth of the GNP each year, defense appropriations have also been increasing, year by year. What do you think of this?

If the GNP increases, defense expenditures should also
  be increased 15%
Defense expenditures should not be increased beyond
  a certain amount, upon which most people can
  agree 46
Defense expenditures should rather be gradually
  decreased 21
Defense expenditures should not be recognized 7
Others; no answer 11

Question 29. The Diet was thrown into confusion over the "securing of appropriations in advance" for the Fourth Defense Power Consolidation Plan and over the shipment of SDF materials to Okinawa. Do you think it will be possible to enforce civilian control over the SDF or do you think this will not be possible in the future?

Can be enforced 16%
Cannot be enforced 18
Don't know 57
Others; no answer 9

Question 30. What do you think of the stationing of the SDF in Okinawa, after its reversion to Japan?

Necessary to station them from the standpoint of
  defense 20%
Necessary to station minimum necessary number of
  personnel in readiness for maintenance of public
  order and safety and for disaster relief activities .. 62
No need to station them at all 12
Others; no answer 6

DOCUMENT 15: EXCERPTS FROM PRESIDENT NIXON'S
1973 REPORT TO CONGRESS, "UNITED STATES FOREIGN
POLICY FOR THE 1970's: SHAPING A DURABLE PEACE"
3 May 1973

Japan

Today we see a new Japan. Her emergence is one of the most striking new features of the international landscape of the 1970s and one of the most dramatic transformations since the period following the Second World War. To speak of Japan's phenomenal economic performance has long been commonplace. Less noted, more recent—and of fundamental importance—is the impact of this power on the international political order. This is a challenge for Japanese policy, for American policy, and for the alliance that binds us together.

*   *   *

In the security field, Japan has for years relied on her treaty with the United States and on the American nuclear deterrent, which freed resources and energies that would otherwise have been required for defense. But she has steadily improved her own conventional defenses, emphasizing modernization rather than size, upgrading her forces in firepower, mobility, and anti-submarine warfare and air defense capability. Her Fourth Defense Plan, for 1972–1976, doubles the expenditure of her Third Plan. This still represents less than 1 percent annually of her Gross National Product, while this Gross National Product has been growing at over 10 percent a year. With the reversion of Okinawa, Japanese forces have now moved southward to take over its defense. These are important steps toward self-reliance and improved capacity for conventional defense of all Japanese territory.

This was an inevitable evolution.

There was no way that Japan and Japan's role in the world could go unaffected by the profound transformation of the international order over the last 25 years. All our alliances have been affected. The recovery and rejuvenation of allies has eroded the rigid bipolar system and given all our allies greater room for independent action. The easing of the Cold War military confrontation has brought other aspects of power—economic, in particular—to the forefront of the international political stage. U.S. military protection no longer suffices as the principal rationale for close partnership and cooperation. In every allied country, leadership has begun to pass to a new generation eager to assert a new national identity at home and abroad.

Japan's emergence is a political fact of enormous importance. Japan is now a major factor in the international system, and her conduct is a major determinant of its stability.

As I have indicated in each of my previous Foreign Policy Reports, I have been concerned since the beginning of this Administration that our alliance relations with Japan had to keep in step with these new conditions. We are faced with new responsibilities toward each other and toward the world. We are challenged to respond to this evolution creatively and together, to keep our alliance on a firm basis in a new era.

For the U.S.-Japanese alliance remains central to the foreign policies of both countries. We are two major powers of the free world, interdependent to an extraordinary degree for our prosperity and our security. The United States therefore places the highest possible value upon the partnership, as it has for more than two decades.

In this year of new commitment to strengthening our ties with Western Europe, I am determined no less to strengthen our alliance with Japan.

* * *

Japan's resurgence from a recipient of American aid into a major economic power and competitor was bound to affect the external political framework which had helped make it possible. In her dealings with the United States, in particular, Japan no longer needed or could afford an almost exclusive concentration on her economic advancement or a habit of acting as a junior partner. She still enjoyed the special advantage that her reliance on the United States for her security freed resources for her economic expansion. The political relationships which continued to safeguard her would require greater reciprocity in her economic relations.

Moreover, Japan was no longer just a regional Pacific power dependent on the United States in the broader diplomatic field. Europe, Asia, North and South America, and Africa were now part of one vast arena of multilateral diplomacy in which Japan was a major factor. Japan was already acting autonomously in an expanding sphere. Her power now brought her new responsibilities. The weight of her economic

160

involvement in the world—her stake in the free world's economic system, her extensive aid programs, and her growing economic ties with Communist powers—would require that she make her decisions on broader policy grounds than economic calculations. We and Japan, as allies, would have to face up to the problem of keeping our independent policies directed at common objectives.

These are the fundamental developments I have sought to address over the last four years. I have sought to adapt our partnership to these transformed conditions of greater equality and multipolar diplomacy. My three meetings with Japanese Prime Ministers, my decision on Okinawa, our discussions of new cooperation in the Far East and in bilateral and multilateral economic areas, and our policies toward China—were all part of this.

The intimacy of the postwar U.S.-Japanese alliance, however, inevitably gave Japan a special sensitivity to the evolution of United States foreign policy. We thus found the paradox that Japan seemed to feel that her reliance on us should limit change or initiatives in American policy, even while she was actively seeking new directions in many dimensions of her own policy. But our abandoning our paternalistic style of alliance leadership meant not that we were casting Japan or any ally adrift, but that we took our allies more seriously, as full partners. Our recognizing the new multipolarity of the world meant not a loss of interest in our alliances, but the contrary—an acknowledgement of the new importance of our allies. American initiatives, such as in China policy or economic policy, were not directed against Japan, but were taken in a common interest or in a much broader context—and in some cases in response to Japanese policies.

The underlying basis of our unity endured. The very centrality of the alliance in Japanese policy was at the heart of the problem. But Japan had to face the implications of her new independence and strength just as the United States was seeking to do. And until this psychological adjustment was fully made by both sides, anomalies in our relations were bound to persist.

This is the background to the events of the past two years and the current public issues facing the U.S.-Japanese alliance.

The Issues on Our Common Agenda

The Economic Dimension. The most urgent issue in U.S.-Japanese relations today is economic—the enormous imbalance in our bilateral trade. We must reduce this imbalance to manageable size in the earliest possible timeframe.

Japan's trade surplus with the United States reflects to a certain extent the competitiveness and productivity of the Japanese economy, as well as the slowness of American exporters to exploit potential markets in Japan. But to a significant degree it has been promoted by anachronistic exchange rates and an elaborate Japanese system of government assistance, complex pricing policies, and restrictions on imports and foreign investment in Japan—vestiges of an earlier period when Japan was still struggling to become competitive with the West. Japan's interest in protecting weaker sectors in her home market is now no different from that of every other nation. The requirement today is a fair system of mutual access to expand trade in a balanced way in both directions. Continued cooperation in dealing with this problem positively is crucial to the ability to fend off growing protectionist pressures and to ensure that the United States is able to address the issues of international trade positively as well. This is a political imperative for both sides.

We believe we have made some progress in the past year.

*　　*　　*

It is no accident that the U.S.-Japan Security Treaty commits our two nations to "seek to eliminate conflict in their international economic policies and . . . encourage economic collaboration between them." Without conscious effort of political will, our economic disputes could tear the fabric of our alliance.

Japan's New Diplomacy. As Japan today moves out in many directions over the terrain of multipolar diplomacy, it will be another test of statesmanship on both sides to ensure that our policies are not divergent. Japan's foreign policy will continue to be shaped by her unique perspectives, purposes, and style. Japan has interests of her own, of which she herself will be the ultimate judge. Our foreign policies will not be identical or inevitably in step. What will preserve our alliance in the new era is not rigidity of policy but a continuing consciousness of the basic interest in stability which we have in common. We must work to maintain a consensus in our policies.

Our respective approaches toward China in 1972 reflected the opportunities and complexities we face, as allies, in the common endeavor of reducing tensions with adversaries.

Japan had for many years been developing economic and cultural contacts with the People's Republic of China when the United States had virtually none. Geography, culture, history, and trade potential have always made China a powerful natural attraction for Japan. Some Japanese criticized the United States for the mutual isolation between the United States and the People's Republic of China, and offered Japan as a natural bridge between the two countries. Today, Japan has full diplomatic relations with the People's Republic, while the United States has not, and Japan's trade with China continues to exceed our own by a wide margin.

*   *   *

. . . there is no inconsistency in principle between our alliance and the new hopeful prospects of relaxation of tension multilaterally. No third country need fear our alliance. Neither Japan nor the United States need fear that our unity precludes a broader community of normalized relations, or independent approaches.

In the years ahead, the kind of close consultation between the United States and Japan which accompanied our respective Peking Summits in 1972 will be critically important to all our diplomatic endeavors. More than our alliance is at stake. Japan has always been conscious of the external global framework within which she was pursuing her own objectives. What is new in the 1970's is her sharing in increased responsibility for it. This responsibility is now implied inescapably in her economic power and her engagement in many directions in global diplomacy.

The complexity of today's geopolitical environment, even in the Asian context alone, is a challenge to a nation of Japan's energy and national spirit undertaking a more active political role. Japan now has the obligations of a major power—restraint, reciprocity, reliability, and sensitivity to her overriding interest in a stable pattern of global relationships.

Today's multilateralism does not diminish the importance of the U.S.-Japanese alliance. On the contrary, our alliance, which has ensured stability in Asia for 20 years, still does, and serves an essential mutual interest in the new conditions. Secured by her alliance with the United States, Japan can engage herself economically and diplomatically in

163

many directions independently, without fearing for her security or being feared by others. It provides a stable framework for the evolution of Japanese policy. This is a general interest.

The U.S.-Japanese alliance in the new era is thus presented with the same challenge as the Atlantic Alliance. We cannot conduct our individual policies on the basis of self-interest alone, taking our alliance for granted. We have an obligation not to allow our short-term policies to jeopardize our long-term unity, or to allow competitive objectives to threaten the common goals of our political association.

Challenges for the Future

Mature countries do not expect to avoid disputes or conflicts of interest. A mature alliance relationship, however, means facing up to them on the basis of mutuality. It means seriously addressing the underlying causes, not the superficial public events. We are now moving in this direction. We must carry it forward.

This means certain obligations on both sides.

In the economic area, the most urgent and divisive area, we both have an obligation to address and solve the common problem of our trade imbalance. We have a responsibility to the international system to normalize the bilateral economic relationship that bulks so large in the international economy. We have an obligation to keep the specific commitments made to each other. We have an opportunity to explore positive approaches to averting clashes in the future. We have a responsibility to provide positive leadership in the urgent efforts at multilateral reform.

In both the political and the economic dimensions, we have an obligation as allies to pursue our individual objectives in ways that serve also our common purposes. Whether the issue be the worldwide energy problem, or economic or political relations with Communist countries, or the provision of resources to developing countries, there are competitive interests necessarily involved, but also an overriding collective interest in a stable global environment. It will require a conscious effort of political will not to make the key decisions according to short-term economic or political advantage. This is more than a problem of bureaucratic management; it is a test of statesmanship.

The United States will be sensitive to Japan's unique perspective on the world and Japan's special relationship with the United States.

To this end, we have redoubled our efforts at consultation. This consultation is institutionalized at several levels and in several channels—through our able Ambassadors; through high-level political consultations such as Dr. Kissinger's three visits to Tokyo in 1972 and 1973; through meetings at the Foreign Minister level such as Mr. Ohira's discussions with Secretary Rogers in Washington in October; through regular Cabinet-level meetings of the Japan-U.S. Committee on Trade and Economic Affairs; and through the three meetings I have had with Japanese Prime Ministers since taking office and the fourth I expect to have this year.

This interchange has a symbolic value in reaffirming a political commitment and also a tangible value in giving it substance.

The same dedication to mutual confidence and close consultation on the part of Japan will be essential as she marks out her independent paths. The complexity of the new diplomacy puts a premium on our steadiness and reliability in all our relationships, particularly with each other.

Japan's foreign policy is for Japan to decide. Both her security and her economic interests, however, link her destiny firmly to that of the free world. I am confident that the political leaders on both sides of the Pacific are deeply conscious of the common interest that our alliance has served, and deeply committed to preserving it.

Cover and book design: Pat Taylor